JUDICIAL ADMINISTRATION OF OTTOMAN EGYPT

STUDIES IN MIDDLE EASTERN HISTORY—NUMBER FOUR

THE JUDICIAL ADMINISTRATION OF OTTOMAN EGYPT IN THE SEVENTEENTH CENTURY

Galal H. El-Nahal

BIBLIOTHECA ISLAMICA
Minneapolis & Chicago
1979

COPYRIGHT

ACKNOWLEDGEMENTS

I owe a special debt of gratitude to Professor Halil Inalcik of the University of Chicago, who was my main source of inspiration and guidance. Any credit for this work is his, but any shortcomings are strictly mine. Many thanks are also due to Professors John Woods and Wilferd Madelung of the University of Chicago, for reading and providing indispensable criticism of the early drafts.

Gratitude and appreciation are also due to the Center for Middle Eastern Studies at the University of Chicago for its grants; the American Research Center in Egypt for supporting my field research in Cairo from 1976 to 1977; the staff of the *Sharī*^{c}*ah* court archives in Cairo; and the director and staff of the Middle East collection at the Joseph Regenstein Library for their assistance in providing the primary and secondary sources.

And finally, a very special thanks to my beloved wife, for all her support. I cannot begin to repay here my enormous debt to her.

CONTENTS

List of Abbreviations viii

Chapter

I. "An Ideal Doctrine for an Ideal Society" 1

II. The Court Registers 9

III. The Composition of the Judiciary 12
- The Courts 12
- The *Qāḍī* ^{c}*Askar* 13
- The Provincial *Qāḍīs* 14
- The *Nā'ibs* 14

IV. Aspects of Court Administration 18
- *Al-Muṣliḥūn* (Arbitrators) 19
- The *Muḥḍirs* 20
- *Ahl al-Khibrah* 22
- The *Muftīs* 23
- The *Rusūm* (Fees) 23

V. Criminal Justice 25
- The Plaintiff 25
- Investigations 26
- Trials 28
- Sentencing 32

VI. Civil Cases 36
- Cases Rejected by the Court 39
- Trials in Absentia 40
- Contempt of Court 40
- Penalties 41
- The Legal Status of Non-Muslims (*Zimmīs*) 42

Chapter

VII. Family Law 44
Divorce by Judicial Decree 46
Inheritance 47
The State and Inheritance 49
The Legal Status of Women 49

VIII. The Role of the Court in Urban Administration . 51
The Population 51
Physical Organization 52
Social Organization 54
Economic Organization 57

IX. Rural Administration and the Administration of the *Awqāf* 65
Rural Administration 65
Administration of the *Awqāf* 68

X. An Ideal Doctrine for a Real Society 72

Appendix

A. The Courts of Cairo and the Provincial Courts . 74
B. The Judicial Hierarchy 76
C. The Registers 77
D. Ottoman Chief Judges in Egypt in the Seventeenth Century 78

Notes 80

Bibliography 100

Index 107

ABBREVIATIONS

This study is derived primarily from seventeenth-century registers of the Cairene courts and one provincial court, housed in the *Sharīᶜah* court archives in Cairo.

Abbreviations for the courts:

BA	al-Bāb al-ᶜĀlī
BF	Banī Sūwayf
BQ	Bāb al-Saᶜādah wa al-Kharq
BR	al-Barmashiyyah
BU	Būlāq
HK	al-Ḥākim
QA	al-Qismah al-ᶜArabiyyah
QR	al-Qismah al-ᶜAskariyyah
QS	Qanāṭir al-Sibāᶜ
QU	Qūṣūn
MQ	Miṣr al-Qadīmah
SH	al-Ṣāliḥiyyah
SA	al-Ṣāliḥ
TU	Ṭūlūn
ZA	al-Zāhid

Other abbreviations:

Annales	*Annales Islamologiques*
BIE	*Bulletin de l'Institut d'Egypte*
BSOAS	*Bulletin of the School of Oriental and African Studies*
EI^2	*Encyclopaedia of Islam*, second revised edition
HJ	*Historia Judaica*
IA	*Islam Ansiklopedisi*

IFM	*Iktisat Fakültesi Mecmuasi* (University of Istanbul)
IS	*Islamic Studies*
IJMES	*International Journal of Middle Eastern Studies*
JAOS	*Journal of the American Oriental Society*
JESHO	*Journal of the Economic and Society History of the Orient*
JTM	*al-Jam^{c}iyyah al-Tārīkhiyyah al-Miṣriyyah* (Egyptian Historical Society)
MTM	*al-Majallah al-Tārīkhiyyah al-Miṣriyyah* (Egyptian Historical Journal)
PIASH	*Proceedings of the Israel Academy of Sciences and Humanities*

Chapter I

"AN IDEAL DOCTRINE FOR AN IDEAL SOCIETY"

The study of law as a system of social control reveals what a society claims to honor and tries to protect. The study of judicial administration discloses whether society in fact protects what it honors, and how. These two questions are of particular importance in the case of Ottoman Egypt (923 A.H./1517-1300 A.H./1882), where the prime instrument of social control was the *Sharīᶜah*.

"An ideal doctrine for an ideal society" is how earlier studies on jurisprudence viewed the *Sharīᶜah*--sacred Muslim law, formulated by jurists on the basis of the revealed word of God. It was understood that the jurists were to analyze the *Sharīᶜah* in abstract terms, and tell the courts only what they *ought* to do. Scholars believed that Muslim law distinguished between the *Sharīᶜah* as formulated by the jurists and the positive law administered in court.[1]

More recently, however, Schacht and others have demonstrated that the process of formulating the *Sharīᶜah* did apply human reasoning to concrete considerations of time and place.[2] Still, the relationship between the theory of the *Sharīᶜah* as pronounced by the jurists and actual practice in courts remains uninvestigated.[3] Court registers from pre-Ottoman periods have not survived, and scholars have had to contend with theoretical works of jurisprudence and the meager information provided by other sources, such as chronicles and biographical dictionaries of *qāḍīs* (judges).

We are somewhat more fortunate. This study is based entirely on court records from seventeenth-century Ottoman Egypt; from these records we may perceive the degree to which the law as administered in the courts diverged from the *Sharīᶜah*. Literary sources from the period, which are particularly limited for the second half of the sixteenth century,[4] are occupied primarily with political events, and from the eighteenth century on, the predominant theme is the struggle between various military factions. Politically, eighteenth-century Egypt was clearly unstable,[5] and though the instability comes late, it tends to influence the historian's view of the entire Ottoman period.

The whole period is seen by most scholars as one of social, economic, and political chaos, before which the Ottoman central authority stood at worst helpless and at best simply indifferent--so long as each year the revenues continued to arrive in Istanbul. The Ottoman government in Egypt was considered exploitative and, by implication, injurious to social and economic order.[6] Egyptian society was conveniently divided by these scholars into two main classes: The Ottoman military, bureaucrats, and ulema formed the tax-exempt and politically active ruling class whose main function (or privilege) was to divert most of the revenues for its maintenance and for the benefit of the government. The taxpaying Egyptians (peasants, artisans, and merchants) formed a submissive subject class whose main duty was to maintain itself at a level of subsistence, and maintain the ruling class in comfort. According to this view, relationships between the two classes were for the most part formal and superficial. Non-Muslims were isolated by the legal and social limitations imposed upon them by the *Sharīᶜah*. The subject class of merchants, artisans, and peasants lived in isolated neighborhoods and villages. The permanently unsettled state of Muslim politics precluded growth of civil spirit and local solidarity and organization (major characteristics of a European medieval society) in Middle Eastern urban centers. The peasants were passive and submissive. While recognizing a few elements of solidarity and civil spirit in the neighborhoods and villages, some scholars ignore the *ṭawā'if* (guilds, sing. *ṭā'ifah*) of artisans and merchants pursuing group aims and economic interests.

In his study of the Muslim cities of Cairo, Damascus, and Aleppo in the later Middle Ages, Lapidus states that

> The population of the markets, however, was very imperfectly organized by comparison with the quarters. Professional, merchant, and artisan guilds were virtually nonexistent, and what rudimentary forms did exist were created by the state for its own purposes rather than by the solidarity and self-interest of the members. The so-called corporations of the physicians, surgeons, and oculists are so

> designated only because chiefs called *ra'īses* were appointed by the state to maintain standards of teaching, practice, and discipline in the professions. There is no indication that these functionaries represented guild solidarities.
>
> Neither were merchants organized into guilds. In the fourteenth century the Karimi merchants in the spice trade between Egypt and India were supervised by a *ra'īs*, selected from their number but appointed by the Sultan to act as a liaison for the organization of their banking, diplomatic, and fiscal duties to the state. . . . The same pattern of close supervision without evident corporate structure also prevailed among the artisanate.[7]

Lapidus then searches for, and finds, the elite ulema as a substitute for the *ṭawā'if*. Because of their family and community ties, their competence, their role in economics, and their political and social interests, the ulema could hold Muslim cities together without recourse to formal institutions of representation or control.[8]

Baer has a somewhat similar view of the guilds in nineteenth-century Egypt. He states that "One of the main characteristics of Egypt's social history is the lack of development of indigenous democratic institutions in that country."[9] He then adds, "In this context it is interesting to discuss the question whether the *shaykh* (head) of the *ṭā'ifah* was elected and freely chosen by the members or appointed by the government,"[10] and decides that, at the time of the French expedition, each *shaykh* was freely elected.[11] Given his earlier claim that the Ottomans had introduced in the sixteenth century an "innovation" whereby the *shaykh* was "appointed" by the *qāḍī*,[12] and his finding of a lack of democratic institutions in Egyptian history, he obviously believes the principle of election was a French innovation.

Egyptian *ṭawā'if* are thus reduced to structures created from above for administrative and fiscal purposes, not voluntary associations established to protect the economic interests of their members.[13] Yet Gibb and Bowen state that the Ottoman government had little or no effect on the institutions and activities of the subject class, and was generally apathetic, arbitrary, and even violent rather than subtle in its dealings with the taxpayers.[14]

In theory, the judiciary could administer every branch of the *Sharīᶜah* and the *qānūns* (secular laws of the Sultan).

In practice, however, military and other executive officials often subjected the taxpayers to illegal levies, or sentenced them to punishment or execution without trial, and in the vast majority of cases were not called to account for their actions.[15]

These views suffer from a lack of information. Few literary sources deal with private citizens and the systems by which they resisted pressures and expressed their interests, or with government systems for maintaining equilibrium in society. Some of these views also reflect unexamined habits of thought about "despotic" Middle Eastern governments and "passive" Middle Eastern societies.

No doubt revenues from taxes were the ultimate goal of Ottoman government in Egypt; the ancient theory of government in the Middle East maintained that the ruler must always endeavor to strengthen his power by expanding his revenues and armies.[16] This theory recognized, however, that wealth and power could only be achieved through justice. The power of the State depended on the army, the army depended on wealth, wealth depended on the prosperity of the taxpayers, and that prosperity depended on justice in taxation and maintenance of social order. The ruler must look after his subjects. He just restrain the powerful from oppressing the weak. He must strive for prosperity in his domain by improving irrigation and communications, and by building new cities.

This ancient theory of government was in many ways similar to that articulated by the Muslim jurists. The most fundamental change was in making observance of the *Sharī^{c}ah* the principal duty of the ruler.[17] Justice, the basis of state power, would prevail if the *Sharī^{c}ah* was upheld, if balance was maintained between the classes, and if every man was kept in his rightful place.

Such a theory of government, as this study will demonstrate, formed the basis of Ottoman government in seventeenth-century Egypt; and the judiciary was the instrument of its implementation. To achieve this, the judiciary had to be kept independent of the military and the other executive branches of government, and it had to be given jurisdiction over all legal and administrative matters. Before the ottoman reforms introduced into Egypt can be fully appreciated, we must briefly survey the judicial system in pre-Ottoman times.

Scholars of Muslim legal history have maintained that in the earlier Islamic states there existed two systems for the administration of justice. The ordinary system administered by the *qāḍī* and based on the *Sharīᶜah* was supplemented by an extraordinary system administered by the ruler and a number of executive officials based on administrative regulations amounting to legislation (*qānūns*). This dichotomy originated in the predominantly private nature of the *Sharīᶜah* and the rigidity of its system of procedure,[18] and was stimulated by Muslim political developments.

Theoretically, the *Sharīᶜah* is all-embracing; it regulates the whole private and public life of Muslims. In reality, Muslim jurists confined themselves mainly to formulating the theory of man's relations with God and his fellow man, and barely touched on the relationship between man and the temporal authority. The *Sharīᶜah* laid down penalties for only six crimes. Murder was a civil offense in which the *qāḍī* could not take action without a formal complaint by the victim's heirs. Moreover, the *Sharīᶜah* imposed a rigid procedure according to which proof could only be established through the testimony of trustworthy *shuhūd* (witnesses, sing. *shāhid*), which impaired the ability of the *qāḍī* to render justice to all people.[19] Effective organization of the affairs of the State and the need to maintain public order therefore required recognition that the ruler had the power both to legislate and to administer justice personally or through executive officials other than the *qāḍī*.[20]

From the time of the Caliph ᶜUmar (13 A.H./634-24 A.H./1644), legal prescriptions and administrative regulations based on the will of the ruler as well as *ᶜurf* (common usage)[21] were incorporated into the *Sharīᶜah* through a broad interpretation of the concept of *sunnah* (tradition) and *istiḥsān* (preference) as sources of the *Sharīᶜah*.[22] In the ninth century, as the sources of the *Sharīᶜah* were defined to exclude *istiḥsān* and narrow down the *sunnah* to the sayings of the prophet, these administrative regulations were left outside the *Sharīᶜah*, and came to constitute the nucleus of an independent, secular *qānūn*.[23]

This process was stimulated by the rise of provincial dynasties and sultans who were challenging the central authority of the Caliphs. Local bureaucrats, particularly in Iran, began to revive the old tradition of State administration in order to consolidate the power of the sultans. Finally, in the Mongol and Turkish traditions of Central Asia, the concept of *qānūn* was firmly established. With the Mongol and later Ottoman invasion of the Middle East, *qānūn* was greatly strengthened.[24] Muslim jurists came to accept the *qānūn* on the basis of *maṣlaḥah* (public interest) and on condition that it supplement but not contradict the *Sharīᶜah*. This principle was known as *al-siyāsah al-sharᶜiyyah* (government in accordance with the sacred law).[25]

The matters regulated by the *qānūn* were those least dealt with by the *Sharīᶜah*, i.e., military and governmental organization, taxation, land law, market supervision, and penal law.[26] The *qānūn*, moreover, was administered by executive officials other than the *qāḍī*.

In Mamluk Egypt (657 A.H./1258-923 A.H./1517), the *qāḍī* heard primarily cases of contracts, debts, and marital disputes involving civilian litigants.[27] A *qāḍī ᶜaskar* (military judge), whose judicial status did not differ from that of the *qāḍī*, heard cases involving military, or military and civilian, litigants.[28] The *qāḍī ᶜaskar*, however, seems to have had concurrent jurisdiction with the *ḥājib* (chamberlain), who was primarily an executive official, over fiscal disputes among the military (i.e., disputes related to *iqṭāᶜ*, the semi-feudal system of land tenure).[29] The *qāḍī* himself had concurrent jurisdiction with the *shurṭah* (police)[30] and the *muḥtasib* (market inspector)[31] over criminal matters. Finally, there existed a superior court of *maẓālim* (appeals or redress), presided over by the ruler himself or his executive agents (governors), with unlimited jurisdiction. The majority of cases heard by the *maẓālim* court were related to abuses of power by officials like tax collectors, and appeals against the *qāḍī*'s decisions.[32]

Unlike the *qāḍī*'s court, which applied the *Sharīᶜah* and was bound by its strict rules of proof, the *maẓālim, shurṭah,* and *muḥtasib* courts applied *qānūns* based on *ᶜurf* and regulations which amounted to sultanic legislation; they were free of the rigid procedure imposed by the *Sharīᶜah*. In other words, confessions could be acquired through force; proof could be established by the testimony of *shuhūd* not legally competent in the *qāḍī*'s courts; cross-examination was allowed; and circumstantial evidence could be admitted.[33]

In the absence of a clear-cut division between the jurisdiction of the ordinary and the extraordinary systems of justice, executive officials gradually encroached upon the domain of the *qāḍī*. This became evident in the fourteenth and fifteenth centuries when the Mamluk central authority was less able to restrain its own executive officials,[34] who in civil and family cases were issuing decisions contradicting the *Sharīᶜah* and thus reducing the authority of the *qāḍī*. Moreover, the lack of formal procedure and the absence of a penal code were conducive to abuse: Confessions were obtained by forcing the defendant to wear a scalding hot pot on his head; and convicts were sentenced to sit on sharpened stakes.[35] In sum, the judicial system in pre-Ottoman Egypt was a dual one: it lacked separation of power; there was no standard system of procedure or penal code for the non-*Sharīᶜah* courts; and the authority of the *qāḍī* had declined markedly.

In 923 A.H./1517 the Ottomans conquered Egypt, brought an end to the Mamluk State, and began a systematic reorganization of the Egyptian administration. Those Mamluks who accepted Ottoman suzerainty were incorporated into the new administration. The *iqṭāᶜ* system of land tenure was abolished and *awqāf* (endowments, sing. *waqf*) not supported by proper documentation were confiscated, thus bringing most of the wealth, both rural and urban, under the direct control of the sultan. Three branches of administration--military, fiscal, and judicial--independent of each other but directly attached to the sultan, were established. A *qānūn* outlining the functions of each branch of government was promulgated in 932 A.H./1525.[36] As the sultan's supreme representative in Egypt, the *wālī* (viceroy) supervised the military, fiscal, and judicial officials and saw to it that they acted according to the *Sharīᶜah* and the *qānūns* of the sultan. This was accomplished in the *Dīwān* (council of government) presided over by the heads of the military, the treasury, and the judiciary.

The main functions of the military, stationed in Cairo and the provinces and attached to the *wālī* and provincial governors, were to defend the country in times of war, to police it in times of peace, to deliver orders, and to assist in the collection of taxes.

The financial branch was in charge of assessing and collecting taxes and expending revenues. Taxes were collected by *amīns* (salaried agents of the treasury) and by *multazims* (tax farmers) in accordance with a tax register compiled by the treasury and kept at each village.

The judiciary was decentralized into a hierarchy independent of the other branches of government. Its functions were to administer the *Sharīᶜah* and the *qānūns* of the sultan in legal, fiscal, and administrative matters. Without a *qāḍī*'s decision, no other official (except the *wālī* as supreme representative of the sultan in Egypt) could subject any individual to punishment or fine. A penal code setting penalties for all crimes was introduced to supplement the *Sharī*ᶜ*ah*. All these measures were aimed at unification of the judicial system, separation of powers, and elimination of abuses of power and corruption by executive officials.

Chapter II
THE COURT REGISTERS

This study is based mainly on registers of the *qāḍīs* housed in the archives of the *Sharīᶜah* courts in Cairo.[1] During the sixteenth and seventeenth centuries, all the cases brought before the *qāḍī*, regardless of their nature, were recorded in a single register. In the eighteenth century, however, separate registers were used for separate areas of law, with a single register for *taqrīr* (the appointment) of the *nāẓirs* (supervisors) of the *awqāf*, for instance, and another for *mubayaᶜāt* (sales).[2]

The numbering system currently used for these registers was assigned in recent times by the Egyptian Ministry of Culture, which now supervises the Archives. The registers are organized into four separate series: al-Bāb al-ᶜĀlī (1-559; abbreviated as BA); al-Qismah al-ᶜAskariyyah (1-418; QR); al-Qismah al-ᶜArabiyyah (1-157; QA); and all other courts (1-717).

The earliest register, from the court of Miṣr al-Qadīmah, begins in 934/1527. It is certain that Miṣr al-Qadīmah and other courts were in operation before the Ottoman conquest, but that some registers were lost. In 1226/1811, Muḥammad ᶜAli reduced the number of courts in Cairo to five. All sub-district courts except for those of al-Bāb al-ᶜĀlī, Būlāq (BU), Miṣr al-Qadīmah (MQ), al-Qismah al-ᶜAskariyyah, and al-Qismah al-ᶜArabiyyah were closed; those five continued in operation until 1292/1875.

The smallest number of registers came from the court of al-Barmashiyyah, where in two and a half centuries, only fifteen registers were compiled, compared with 519 registers at the court of al-Bāb al-ᶜĀlī (see Appendix C). Although from gaps between the registers it is certain that a few registers were lost, al-Barmashiyyah clearly did not have much business. The scribe of the court lamented his misfortune (the income of the scribes came from fees collected on transactions notarized in court) on the front page of a register: "Al-Barmashiyyah is pleasant in its hall and setting, scanty in its gold, silver, and money."[3]

The registers are 40 by 50 centimeters and average 500 pages; each contains as many as two to three thousand cases heard over one to two years. A typical well-preserved register begins with the names of the *qāḍīs* presiding over the court; at the court of al-Bāb al-ᶜĀlī, the list was headed by the Ottoman *qāḍī ᶜaskar* (chief justice), followed by the Ḥanafī *nā'ib* (magistrate), and, finally, at the bottom, by the Shāfiᶜī, Mālikī, and Ḥanbalī *nā'ibs* listed next to each other.

According to a directive from the *qāḍī ᶜaskar* to the various courts, the cases were supposed to be recorded daily by the *ᶜudūl* (notaries). Occasionally, however, the *ᶜudūl* apparently accumulated the documents of several trials over a week or more, and as a result confusion occurred in the recording.[5]

Because the cases were summarized and recorded by a number of *ᶜudūl*, the handwriting changed frequently. Deciphering the script is sometimes possible only because cliches were often used. Indeed, there existed in Islamic law a branch of literature called *shurūṭ* (terms) which instructed the *ᶜudūl* on formulas to be used in contracts.

The court in Ottoman Egypt had jurisdiction over all disputes related to criminal, family, and civil laws. The court also functioned as an administrative center, hearing cases related to building regulations, taxation, urban and provincial administration, and the administration of *awqāf*. Letters and administrative directives from the *wālī* and the *qāḍī ᶜaskars* were generally recorded at the front or back of each register in Turkish, and summarized in Arabic.

Finally, various sales in commodities and urban properties, loans, manumissions of slaves, marriages, divorces, and conversions to Islam were all notarized in court. Although Islamic law did not require that contracts and transactions be written to be valid (the law required only that they be witnessed by at least two *shuhūd*), transactions were commonly notarized in court. Having transactions witnessed in court provided security in case of future disputes. The integrity of the *ᶜudūl* was supposedly beyond any doubt (unlike private *shuhūd*, whose integrity could always be suspect). Moreover, they were trained in the *shurūṭ* and could record the transactions so as to conform to the letter of the *Sharīᶜah*, whether or not the transaction was legal. (The practice of using legal means to achieve extra-legal ends was known as *ḥiyal*.) Finally, although the documents themselves did not constitute evidence and did not give rise to legal obligation, they helped to preserve the terms of the contract.

Because the functions of Ottoman Egyptian courts were so broad, the registers are invaluable as a source of information on the social and legal history of Egypt; but certain limitations must be kept in mind. Egyptian society was (and still is) traditional to some degree. Loyalties to families, clans, and tribes were strong. In such a society, people seek the help of the state in their disputes only as a last resort. It must be assumed that many disputes were settled within the family, the tribe, or the community according to custom, and therefore did not appear before the court. Moreover, in Islamic law the *qāḍī* was not supposed to act upon crimes of battery or murder unless a formal complaint was made by the victim or his representative. (The state did press murder charges when the victim left no heirs.) This may explain the relatively small number of crimes found in the registers.

In criminal cases, the registers tend not to detail the punishment, either because penalties were codified or because the cases were summarized. In commercial cases, the use of formulas in writing contracts makes it very difficult to assess the degree to which commercial practices conformed to the *Sharīᶜah*. Other aspects of the administration of justice not clear on the basis of the documents examined will be discussed below.

The data presented here are drawn from a limited number of registers, randomly selected (because of the large number of registers and the absence of indexes). The registers were chosen so as to cover as much of the seventeenth century as possible. Moreover, while most of the documents examined came from the court of al-Bāb al-ᶜĀlī, because it was the main court in Cairo, documents from other Cairene courts and one provincial court were also examined for the sake of comparison. Still, this study must be considered to be more indicative than comprehensive.

Chapter III

THE COMPOSITION OF THE JUDICIARY

In this chapter we will examine the courts of Ottoman Egypt; the functions of the *qāḍī ᶜaskar*, the provincial *qāḍīs*, and the *nā'ibs*; and the relationship between the *qāḍīs* and the *nā'ibs* in each district, the *nā'ibs* in each court, and the judiciary and other executive officials.

THE COURTS

For financial and administrative purposes, Egypt was divided into twenty-four provinces.[1] For the purpose of judicial administrative, each province was divided into one or more *qaḍā's* (judicial districts), with a court in each.[2] There were thirty-seven main *qaḍā's* altogether.[3] Each main *qaḍā'* was divided into *nāḥiyyahs* (sub-districts), with a court in each. The city of Cairo constituted one *qaḍā'* under the jurisdiction of the *qāḍī ᶜaskar*, but was further divided into at least fifteen[4] *nāḥiyyahs*, presided over by *nā'ibs*. The total number of *nāḥiyyahs* throughout Egypt is not known.[5]

The courts were organized into a hierarchy of six grades through which the *qāḍīs* were promoted.[6] The ranking system was based on revenues, with the largest revenue-producing courts ranking highest.[7] Each *nāḥiyyah* administered both *Sharīᶜah* and *qānūns*, except for matters of inheritance.[8] This aspect of the *Sharīᶜah* was placed from the outset of the Ottoman era in Egypt under the exclusive jurisdiction of two courts, al-Qismah al-ᶜAskariyyah, for inheritances left by members of the military and the bureaucracy, and al-Qismah al-ᶜArabiyyah, for inheritances left by private citizens.[9] Cases of inheritance originating in the provinces were administered by the local courts under the supervision of a representative of one of the Qismahs.[10]

All the courts of Cairo except the court of al-Bāb

al-ᶜĀlī, which was in a palace,[11] were associated with mosques.[12] Just where they were located in the mosque, however, is not known. Mīlād suggests that the trials were conducted in the *īwāns*, which open on the courtyard of the mosque through arcades.[13] Her view is that, since all the mosques used for the courts contained four *īwāns* and each court was presided over by four *nā'ibs*, each *nā'ib* would occupy a single *īwān*.[14]

THE *QĀḌĪ ᶜASKAR*

The head of the judiciary in Egypt was known as *qāḍī al-quḍāh* (judge of judges) or as *qāḍī ᶜaskar*.[15] The latter was an honorary title, out of respect for Egypt's former position as a seat of the caliphate and because the first man to occupy the post was the *qāḍī ᶜaskar* of the conquering Ottoman army.[16]

During the seventeenth century, approximately eighty foreign *qāḍī ᶜaskars*[17] were sent to Egypt to preside over the judicial administration.[18] The *qāḍīs* of the main cities of the empire including Cairo were appointed from a list drawn up by the chief *muftī* (jurist) and submitted to the sultan for confirmation.[19] Theoretically, promotion to such high posts was made from among the teachers of the highest schools of the empire on the basis of seniority.[20] In reality, other factors were equally important. During the seventeenth century, when demand for high positions like the judgeship of Cairo was far higher than the number available,[21] proximity to key figures like the sultan or the chief *muftī* was an important factor in promotion.[22] Indeed, many of the Egyptian *qāḍī ᶜaskars* belonged to families of prominent ulema, and some were related to the grand *muftī* or *qāḍī ᶜaskars* in Istanbul.[23] Gifts which amounted to bribes were also used to secure promotion.[24] The *wālī* in Egypt normally had nothing to do with the appointment of the *qāḍī ᶜaskar*, although if the *qāḍī ᶜaskar* died before his term expired, the *wālī* could appoint a *qā'im maqām* (substitute) until the new *qāḍī ᶜaskar* arrived.[25] In one such case, the *wālī* appointed a *qā'im maqām* and sent a petition on his behalf to Istanbul. The *qā'im maqām* was confirmed and served as *qāḍī ᶜaskar*.[26]

Qāḍī ᶜaskars were appointed to one-year terms, but a few served two and three terms, with or without intervals.[27] The *qāḍī ᶜaskar* functioned as chief justice of Egypt and *qāḍī* of the district of Cairo. As chief justice, he sat, along with the treasurer and the heads of the military corps, in the *Dīwān*.[28] As the *qāḍī* of Cairo, he presided over the court of al-Bāb al-ᶜĀlī.[29]

THE PROVINCIAL *QĀḌĪS*

Each main *qaḍā'* in Egypt was presided over by an Ottoman *qāḍī* appointed for a term of two years by the *qāḍī ᶜaskar* of Anatolia, on the recommendation of the *qāḍī ᶜaskar* of Egypt.[30] According to the seventeenth-century biographer al-Muḥibbī, many *qāḍī ᶜaskars* moved from one post to another with a number of students and followers, whom they appointed as *qāḍīs* and *nā'ibs* wherever they went.[31] He also mentions one case in which a provincial *qāḍī* was appointed through the help of the *wālī*.[32]

The *qāḍīs* of al-Qismah al-ᶜAskariyyah and al-Qismah al-ᶜArabiyyah, known as *al-Qassāms* (trustees), were also appointed directly by the *qāḍī ᶜaskar* of Anatolia,[33] upon the recommendation of the *qāḍī ᶜaskar* of Egypt.[34] Indeed, during the first half of the eighteenth century, it was common to find Egyptian *qāḍī ᶜaskars* functioning also as *qassāms*.[35] In some cases, the sons of the *qāḍī ᶜaskars* were appointed *qassāms*.[36]

THE *NĀ'IBS*

The Ḥanafī school of jurisprudence was the official school of the empire, and the *qāḍī ᶜaskar* and the provincial *qāḍīs* were Ḥanafīs. Each *qāḍī*, however, appointed *nā'ibs* (Shāfiᶜī, Mālikī, Ḥanbalī, and at times a Ḥanafī) in each court in his district.[37]

The *nā'ibs* were mostly Egyptians,[38] but a few were non-Egyptians who came with the *qāḍī ᶜaskar* and were appointed by him. For example, Muḥammad b. ᶜAbd al-Ḥalīm, *qāḍī ᶜaskar* in 1649-50, appointed his brother Musṭāfa the Ḥanafī *nā'ib* at al-Bāb al-ᶜĀlī.[39] According to al-Muḥibbī, when Yaḥyā b. Zakariyyā (*qāḍī ᶜaskar* of Egypt in 1009 A.H./1600-1010 A.H./1601) was appointed to Damascus, he took with him eleven of his and his father's students, whom he appointed there as his *nā'ibs*.[40] He brought six of them to Egypt and installed them in Cairo.[41] The *nā'ibs* (except for the Ḥanafī *nā'ib* at the court of al-Bāb al-ᶜĀlī, who always left with the *qāḍī ᶜaskar*) were appointed for life. From 1060 A.H./1650 to 1083 A.H./1672, the Shāfiᶜī,

Mālikī, and Hanbalī *nā'ibs* were the same at the court of al-Bāb al-ᶜAlī for most of the period.[42] The only change was in 1063 A.H./1653, when the Ḥanbalī *nā'ib* ᶜUthmān al-Futūḥī died and was replaced by his son, Aḥmad al-Futūḥī.[43] The latter died in 1083 A.H./1672 and was replaced by his brother, Muḥammad al-Futūḥī.[44] The Futūḥī family monopoly over this post is not unique,[45] but the degree of the phenomenon is not yet known.

The point to remember is that the sultan was the sole source of both executive and judicial authority, and that the entire judiciary in Egypt received its authority from him whether directly or indirectly. The *wālī* in Egypt (who was also appointed by the sultan), and his subordinate provincial governors had to do with the appointment of *qādīs* only in extraordinary situations. This separation of powers enabled the judiciary to perform its functions free of military influence. The Ottoman penal code stated that the main function of the *qādī* was to prevent oppression by the military.[46] The *qānūn* of Egypt stated that governors should not adjudicate cases themselves but should refer them to the *qādīs*, and that no one should under any circumstances be subjected to punishment without a *qādī's* decision.[47] *Qāḍīs* unable to prevent the military from oppressing subjects were to inform the central authority. Failure to do so would cause the *qāḍī's* dismissal.[48] A majority of the members of the *Dīwān*, to which the *qādī ᶜaskar* belonged,[49] could suspend any other member, including the *wālī*, if he was found to have acted against the *qānūn*.[50] The *qādī ᶜaskar*, moreover, was appointed by *berāt* (official decree), and as such was entitled to write directly to the sultan and receive letters directly in his name.[51] Egypt's *qānūn* also gave the *qādī ᶜaskar* and provincial *qāḍīs* the right to suspend district financial officers who were convicted of misconduct, and to propose a replacement and inform the central authority of the action.[52] The *qādīs* were also to inform the central authority if they could not prevent the governors from oppressing the subjects.[53]

The *qāḍīs* were not free, however, from all checks over their functions. The *wālī* could imprison the *qāḍī* if he was found to take sides with the guilty and did not act justly,[54] or sold offices to the *nā'ibs*.[55]

The system relied, however, on the honesty and courage of the members of the judiciary. Letters sent by the *qāḍī ᶜaskar* to the *nā'ibs* in the various courts stated that the purpose of the judiciary was to serve the interests of the subjects[56] and that members of the judiciary must be God-fearing and should not obstruct justice by neglecting the interests of the subjects.[57]

The internal independence of the judiciary was equally important for the impartial application of the *qānūn*. Although the *qāḍīs* appointed the *nā'ibs* in their districts, the office of the *nā'ibs*, who served for life, was not attached to that of the *qāḍīs*, who had one or two-year terms. In this respect, although the *nā'ibs* were deputies of the *qāḍīs* who appointed them, in a larger context they were also *nā'ibs* of the sultan. The *nā'ibs* adjudicated cases independently from the *qāḍīs*. Each case was usually presided over by a single *nā'ib*,[58] but those which involved litigants belonging to two different schools of jurisprudence were presided over by more than one.[59]

The *qāḍīs* did exercise some authority over their *nā'ibs*, acting as overseers of the *nā'ibs*' conduct. For example, when it was reported to the *qāḍī* of Cairo that the *nā'ibs* were overcharging for court services, he instructed the courts regarding the fees to be collected and how they should be distributed. His orders always ended with a warning that violators would be severely punished.[60]

Nā'ibs could not accept cases related to *ījārāt* (long-term rentals) or *istibdāl* (replacement) of *awqāf*, *iflās* (bankruptcy), and *faskh* (abrogation of marriage contracts), which were to be referred only to the court of al-Bāb al-ᶜĀlī[61]--and even there, the *nā'ibs* were not allowed to adjudicate such cases without the permission of the *qāḍī*. Finally, *nā'ibs* who wished a leave of absence had to apply to the *qāḍī* for permission.[62]

In each sub-district court the Ḥanafī *nā'ib* had a more important role than the other three. In the registers, his name on the front page is often alone and above the others.[63] A document from the court of al-Bāb al-ᶜĀlī described the order of a court in session as follows: the *qāḍī ᶜaskar* sat in the very front of what must have been a rather large hall. Behind him sat a number of *ᶜudūl*, forming a circle, *al-rukn al-mustadīr* (the circular corner). Behind them sat the Ḥanafī *nā'ib*, alone, with his *ᶜudūl* forming a row (*al-ṣaff al-qaṣīr*, the short row) leaning toward him. Finally, the Shāfiᶜī, Mālikī, and Ḥanbalī *nā'ibs*, with their *ᶜudūl* behind them, sat at the very end, forming what was called *al-ṣaff al-mustadīm* (the regular row).[64] On orders from the *qāḍī ᶜaskar*, the *ᶜudūl* were not allowed to issue documents outside the court without the knowledge and permission of the Ḥanafī *nā'ib*,[65] who was the authority (*al-marji*ᶜ) in each court; control of the revenues of the court was his responsibility.[66]

The Ḥanafī was the official school of the empire. The Ḥanafī *nā'ibs* in Cairo came with the *qāḍī* ᶜ*askar* as relatives or students, and left with him; they thus might be expected to cooperate with the *qāḍī*. As outsiders, they could be detached from the locale over which they were to administer justice.

In sum, Egypt was divided for administrative and fiscal purposes into a number of provinces, each headed by a governor. Each province was divided for purposes of judicial administration into *qaḍā's*, each presided over by an Ottoman *qāḍī*, and the *qaḍā's* were further divided into *nāḥiyyahs*, presided over by *nā'ibs*.

Internally, the judiciary was organized into a hierarchy of ranks, but for promotional purposes only. Each *qāḍī* or *nā'ib* administered justice independently, but certain cases like abrogation of marriage contracts, long-term rentals of endowed properties, replacement of endowed properties, and bankruptcy, were reviewed by the *qāḍī* before being adjudicated by a *nā'ib*. Each case was presided over by a single *qāḍī* or *nā'ib*, unless the litigants belonged to different schools of jurisprudence. The *qāḍī* in the *qaḍā'* and the Ḥanafī *nā'ib* in each court exercised administrative authority over the *nā'ibs* under them in matters of appointment, discharge, collection and distribution of fees, and permissions to conduct business outside the court.

Externally, the entire judiciary, from top to bottom, was appointed independently from the *wālī* and the provincial governors, except in extraordinary circumstances such as the sudden death of a *qāḍī*. According to Ottoman *qānūn*, executive officials could not subject any individual to punishment or fines without a *qāḍī's* decision. The degree to which this rule was applied will be investigated in the following chapters.

Chapter IV

ASPECTS OF COURT ADMINISTRATION

Testimony by *shuhūd* was the most important institution within the Islamic system of proof. The plaintiff had to provide *shuhūd*, the number varying according to the nature of the case, to testify in support of his claims. Although written testimony was often presented in civil, family, and administrative disputes, it did not by itself constitute evidence. When such testimony, including *ḥujjahs* (documents) issued by the courts, was presented, the *qāḍī* always demanded that *shuhūd* testify to the validity of the contents.[1] This emphasis on testimony by *shuhūd* posed a threat to the administration of justice as well as to the legality of transactions, because the *shuhūd* could always be suspected and discarded, and thus the practice of testimony by the *ᶜudūl* was established to insure that justice would not be jeopardized.[2] Individuals whose reliability and integrity had been investigated and confirmed by the *qāḍī* could be installed as accredited *ᶜudūl*, whose testimony could not be suspected or discredited.[3]

The letters of appointment and the orders of the *qāḍī ᶜaskar*[4] to the various courts always emphasized that the *ᶜudūl* must be God-fearing and should strive to protect public and private interests.[5] Any *ᶜudūl* who were convicted of fraud or illicit dealings were dismissed, and the various courts were instructed not to hire them.[6]

Of the nineteen *ᶜudūl* at the court of al-Bāb al-ᶜĀlī, thirteen sat behind the *qāḍī ᶜaskar*, two behind the Ḥanafī *nā'ib*, and four behind the other three *nā'ibs*.[7]

The main functions of the *ᶜudūl* were to notarize and issue *ḥujjahs* for all legal transactions made in court. Each *ḥujjah* begins with the name of the *qāḍī* before whom it was issued and ends with the names of the *ᶜudūl* who witnessed it.[8] Each *ḥujjah* had to be witnessed by at least two *ᶜudūl*,[9] or it could not be considered as evidence in court[10]; some were witnessed by as many as twelve *ᶜudūl*.[11] Trials were also witnessed by the *ᶜudūl*, who issued a notarized record of them.[12] When *ḥujjahs* or records of trials were presented as evidence, the *ᶜudūl* who notarized them were called upon to testify to the contents.

The *ᶜudūl* also assisted the *qāḍī* in investigations made outside the court, and confirmed to the *qāḍī* the integrity of *shuhūd* presented by the litigants as eyewitnesses to crimes or transactions. The *shuhūd* could be military[13] or civilians,[14] Muslims[15] or non-Muslims,[16] males or females.[17] Muslim *shuhūd* could testify for and against Muslims or non-Muslims,[18] non-Muslims only in cases involving other non-Muslims.[19] The testimony of two women counted as one witness.[20]

The integrity of the *shuhūd* was supposed to be confirmed before they could testify in court.[21] This process of *al-taᶜdīl al-sharᶜī* (confirmation of the integrity of the *shuhūd* in accordance with the *Sharīᶜah*),[22] was effected through testimony before the *qāḍī* by two individuals.[23] The latter were in some cases *ᶜudūl*,[24] but could be soldiers,[25] ulema,[26] or artisans and merchants[27] residing in the neighborhood of the *shuhūd*, who were for these purposes called *ᶜudūl al-nāḥiyyah*.[28] This suggests that, in addition to the *ᶜudūl* of the court, individuals of confirmed integrity from among the notables of each locality were installed to testify to the trustworthiness of *shuhūd* from their own areas. This would be a reasonable assumption, since the limited number of official *ᶜudūl* surely could not testify for all the *shuhūd* brought to court.[29]

AL-MUṢLIḤŪN (ARBITRATORS)

People who acted as arbitrators in trials were called interchangeably *al-muslimūn* or *al-muṣliḥūn*.[30] It is not clear who these people were and how they were related to the courts. Appointment of other members of the court staff was often recorded in the registers, but there is not one single letter of appointment of a *muṣlih* or a *muslim*. A document which described the order of the court while in session did not mention the *muṣliḥs* or the *muslims*; nor did the orders of the *qāḍī ᶜaskars* to the various courts which gave instructions with respect to rules and regulations.[31] Finally, the names of arbitrators and their signatures never appeared in the registers.[32] Occasionally it is stated that *al-muṣliḥūn* have intervened and reconciled differences between the litigants--usually when the plaintiff had failed to provide evidence against the defendant.[33] There is no evidence that the *muṣliḥūn* had any official status or served as advisors to the *qāḍīs*.[34] The documents occasionally mention that litigants brought to the court people (possibly neighbors or associates) as *muslims*, who attended the trial.[35] Since the trials were usually open to the public, the *muṣliḥūn* may have come from among those who attended, whether out of curiosity or personal interest in a particular case.

In some cases, "*al-muslimūn*" was used to designate people introduced by the litigants as *shuhūd* to crimes and disputes.[36] Also, cases investigated outside by *ᶜudūl* of the court (such as murder, battery, and theft) often entailed questioning people in the area where the crime had taken place; these people were often called the *muslims* from among the people of the neighborhood, and their names were given.[37] Among them were members of the military, *qāḍīs*, and people who were simply residents of the area where the crime took place.[38] All this suggests that *al-muslimūn* were not a fixed group, but were individuals without any official status who attended trials and acted as reconciliators, or mere witnesses present at the scene of the crime.

THE *MUḤḌIRS*

Each court was staffed with *muḥḍirs* (bailiffs), retired members of the military court appointed by the *qāḍī ᶜaskar* of Egypt or of Anatolia.[39] Uniformed *muḥḍirs* were supposed to stand in front of the court with a bamboo stick in hand, ready to summon defendants to the court upon the request of the plaintiffs or, in cases referred to the court by the *wālī*, of the *qāḍī*.[40] Letters circulated by the *qāḍī ᶜaskar* which state that the *muḥḍirs* should not obstruct justice by neglecting their duties or by refusing to help poor people bring defendants to court[41] hint that the *muḥḍirs* were occasionally amenable to bribes from the defendants. The letters also told the *muḥḍirs* not to collect any fees from the litigants (the *muḥḍirs'* fees came out of court revenues[42]), and not to take part in trials.[43]

The registers, however, are vague on the extent of the *muḥḍir*'s authority with respect to summoning defendants. Usually the defendant sent for responded obediently[44];

although a defendant might be summoned several times before he actually came to court.[45] Arrest or use of force is not mentioned. Such cases suggest that the *muḥḍir* was not supposed to arrest defendants or force them to come; arrest was usually made by the police or by a janissary.

If a murder took place in a neighborhood or a village, under the Ottoman penal code, people in the vicinity were responsible for arresting the criminal or paying blood money. If thefts occurred in public places like baths or in the neighborhoods, the bath attendant or the guard assigned to the neighborhood[46] or people nearby at the time of the crime were responsible for finding the stolen items or paying compensation.[47]

Most cases, however, began with the plaintiff making charges against the defendant, who was always present, but details of how the latter was arrested and by whom were not recorded.[48] If the victim of homicide was a slave, the owner of the slave pressed charges.[49] If the murder victim was without heirs, the viceroy appointed the *amīn bayt al-māl* (the head of the department in charge of the property of deceased individuals without heirs), to press charges.[50] Defendants accused of apostasy after conversion to Islam were accused by private individuals.[51] In those cases involving accusations of misconduct by a resident of a neighborhood, charges were usually made by a number of his neighbors.[52]

The person who made the charges was usually the person who arrested the defendant, and if the defendant did not come, plaintiffs could resort to the *muḥḍir*. A few cases indicate that plaintiffs occasionally resorted to the *ṣūbāshī* (chief of police) or to a member of the military corps[53] to arrest defendants.[54] In such cases, a fee called *ḥaqq al-ṭarīq* was collected from the defendant by the official making the arrest.[55] It seems that the practice was occasionally abused. Individuals in collaboration with the police would arrest innocent persons for the sole purpose of collecting *ḥaqq al-ṭarīq*, which was probably split between them.[56] In one case where the defendant was proven innocent, the *qāḍī* ordered the plaintiff to reimburse the defendant for *ḥaqq al-ṭarīq*.[57] If the plaintiff refused, he was to be imprisoned until he promised to pay.[58] But in another case, the *qāḍī* warned a woman plaintiff that if she had the innocent defendant arrested again, she would have to pay *ḥaqq al-ṭarīq* herself.[59]

The amount of *ḥaqq al-ṭarīq* varied from one case to another (possibly in relation to the distance the defendant lived from court), but it was arbitrary and was often over-estimated. Once when a defendant was residing in Cairo, *ḥaqq al-ṭarīq* was seventeen *niṣfs* (silver *paras*),[60] but in another case when the defendant was brought from al-Fayūm in Upper Egypt to Cairo, *ḥaqq al-ṭarīq* was four thousand *niṣfs*.[61] The defendant was acquitted and the *qāḍī* ordered the plaintiff to refund the *ḥaqq al-ṭarīq*.[62]

AHL AL-KHIBRAH

Ahl al-khibrah were professionals appointed by the court to give a learned opinion in a single case or to conduct a certain investigation which the *qāḍī* or the *ᶜudūl* alone could not handle. Cases requiring physical examination of women were handled by a woman appointed by the *qāḍī*. For example, a plaintiff father claimed that he had married his minor daughter to the defendant on condition that he would not have sexual intercourse with her for three years from the date of the contract, but that the defendant broke the contract, causing his daughter to become ill. The husband admitted the intercourse, but denied causing the girl to become ill. The plaintiff requested that the girl be examined by a woman (referred to in the document as a *qāḍī*) appointed by the court. The expert confirmed the allegations. The father asked the defendant to divorce his wife, and the defendant complied.[63]

Ahl al-khibrah were frequently appointed in disputes related to violations of building codes, like building a house that blocked the way of the neighbors, putting in new doors or windows that violated the privacy of others, or placing heavy equipment in an apartment that threatened the safety of the building. In such cases, a member of the *ṭā'ifah* of the builders was sent along with the *ᶜudūl* to investigate and make recommendations. Builders were also called upon to give learned opinions in disputes related to *awqāf*. The *nāẓir* of the *wafq* was supposed to appropriate as much money from the revenues of the *waqf* as was necessary for the maintenance of the property. Such funds were often the subject of disputes between the *nāẓirs* and the beneficiaries who received the balance of the *waqf* revenues. In such cases, the *qāḍī* appointed a builder to estimate reasonable costs of maintenance.

Division of estates often called for appointment of *ahl al-khibrah* to appraise or supervise the sale of the property. In most of these cases, *ahl al-khibrah* were *shaykhs* or members of the *ṭawā'if* engaged in the production or marketing of similar products. (*Shaykhs* were also consulted in disputes between members of the *ṭawā'if*.) In cases of inheritance, *ahl al-khibrah* were paid fees for their services, which were charged against the inheritance before the division was made. In other cases, nothing is mentioned about the fees of *ahl al-khibrah*, but it is likely that they were also paid by the litigants.

THE *MUFTĪS*

Though not part of the court's regular staff, the *muftīs* had functions closely related to administration of the law. The main function of the *muftīs* was to give *fatwahs* (opinions) on points of the law not dealt with by the *Sharī^cah*, upon the request of individuals. Theoretically, the *fatwahs* were advisory only and did not have the force of law,[64] but in the few cases in which *fatwahs* were issued, they were requested by the *qāḍī*.

THE *RUSŪM* (FEES)

According to the registers, the courts were supposed to collect sixty *niṣfs* for notarizing the marriage of a virgin, thirty for the marriage of a widow or a divorcee,[65] and fifteen for issuing other *ḥujjahs*.[66] These revenues were distributed among the staff. The *ᶜudūl* received four *niṣfs* for issuing a deed and one for recording it in the registers. The *muḥḍir* received one *niṣf* for each *ḥujjah* and the balance went to the *qāḍī* or the *nā'ib*.[67]

Orders from the *qāḍī ᶜaskars* to the *nā'ibs* and the *ᶜudūl* instructing them not to charge more than the *rusūm* listed warned that violators would be subjected to severe punishment.[68]

The fees apparently reached some two million *niṣfs* per year,[69] and the *qāḍī ᶜaskar* also received twenty *ardabbs* of wheat[70] and the same quantity of barley per day from the imperial granary.[71] On his arrival in Egypt, the *qāḍī* distributed cash and clothes to the staff of the court.[72]

In sum, there were four types of witnesses: (1) *Al-ʿudūl*, on the staff of the court, who observed court procedure, notarized *ḥujjahs*, and functioned as assistants to the *qāḍīs*. The *ʿudūl* were paid fees by the court for their services. (2) *ʿUdūl* who were not part of the court staff, whose integrity had previously been confirmed, and who were brought forth to testify to the trustworthiness of eyewitnesses. (3) *Al-muṣliḥūn* and *al-muslimūn*, a group of people without formal status who attended trials and voluntarily mediated differences between litigants in cases which could not be prosecuted. (4) Finally, the *shuhūd* testified on behalf of litigants as eyewitnesses to crimes and disputes rather than as witnesses to procedure in court. The reliability of *shuhūd* was supposed to be confirmed through the testimony of *ʿudūl* before they could testify.

Finally, each court was staffed by *muḥḍirs* whose main duty was to summon the defendants to court, but who had no authority to arrest defendants. *Ahl al-khibrah* were appointed by the court to give testimony in cases requiring expert opinions. The main function of the *muftīs*, who were not part of the staff of the court, was to give *fatwahs* on legal matters not dealt with by the *Sharīʿah*.

Chapter V

CRIMINAL JUSTICE[1]

Criminal cases heard by the court included verbal assault, battery, abduction, theft, murder, fornication, false accusation of fornication, rape, drinking of alcohol, non-attendance at public prayers, apostasy, and misconduct. There were not many criminal cases. In one register from the court of al-Bahnasa, covering five hundred cases in approximately one year, less than 3 per cent were criminal: There were only three cases of murder, one of rape, one case of false accusation of fornication, four cases of battery, three cases of verbal assault, and one case in which some women were accused of misconduct.[2]

THE PLAINTIFF

The *Sharīʿah* defines two types of crimes: those chiefly violating *ḥuqūq Allāh* (the rights of God), including fornication, false accusation of fornication, apostasy, drinking of alcohol, theft, highway robbery, murder, and physical injury; and offenses violating *ḥuqūq al-ākharīn* (the rights of individuals).[3] Theoretically, the *qāḍī* could not act in cases involving *ḥuqūq al-ākharīn* unless a request was made by the victim himself or his representative, but if the *ḥuqūq Allāh* had been violated, the *qāḍī* could act upon his own initiative. The Ḥanafī school, however, held that the *qāḍī* could not act upon his own initiative in any case. In reality, most cases were brought upon the request of the victim himself, his next of kin, his representative, or a state official such as the *wālī*, the *ṣūbāshī*, or the *multazim*.[4] Cases of fornication, false accusation of fornication, rape and sexual offenses, battery, verbal assault, theft, and kidnapping were always brought by the victim or his next of kin, if the victim could not be present.[5] The use of a *wakīl* was limited in criminal cases but quite common in marital disputes and litigation related to contracts and debts.[6] In murder cases, the victim's next of kin usually pressed charges against the defendant.[7] If the victim was a slave, the slave-owner pressed charges,[8] and if the victim left no heirs, the *wālī* appointed an official to press charges.[9] Cases involving apostasy, accusation of drinking of liquor, non-attendance at public prayers, and misconduct were also brought upon the complaint of private individuals or officials like the guard of the neighborhood.[10] It was not uncommon either to find an individual confessing of his own free will to committing a serious crime such as fornication, and demanding to be punished.[11]

The *qāḍī* had the power to act independently in certain cases on his own knowledge and authority, as when he discharged an *ᶜudūl* for giving false testimony or issuing illegal *ḥujjahs*, without a formal complaint.[12] The *qāḍī* also (see p. 62) occasionally toured the market to inspect weights, measures, and prices, and tried those found in violation of the rules, although these violations might also be brought to court by the *muḥtasib*.

It is not clear from the registers whether charges were made orally or in writing.[13] Cases presented to the *wālī* were put in writing before they were referred to the *qāḍī*.[14] A similar procedure may have been followed in the courts, with the plaintiff dictating his charges to the *ᶜudūl*, who in turn presented it to the *qāḍī*.

INVESTIGATIONS

If the plaintiff could bring the defendant to court, the case was tried immediately. If the criminal managed to escape, the court first investigated. Requests for investigation were usually made by the victim himself in cases of theft,[15] or by the complainant, whether the victim or his successor in interest,[16] in cases of battery and murder.[17] Crimes were sometimes reported directly to the *wālī*, who then requested investigation by the court.[18]

Upon request, two *ᶜudūl*, sometimes accompanied by a *qāḍī*, the *wālī*'s messenger, or the person who had reported the case, were sent to the scene of the crime to investigate and report.[19] In cases of theft, the investigators searched for clues to how entrance was made, items stolen were listed with the help of the victim, and the *ᶜudūl* questioned bystanders for possible suspects.[20] In cases of murder[21] or death by accident,[22] the investigators examined the corpse, verified the cause of death, questioned bystanders about possible suspects, and reported to the court after ordering burial.

Accusations of misconduct by a neighbor were also investigated: A group of residents of the area of Ṭūlūn complained to the *wālī* that a neighbor had a habit of inviting strange men and women to his house, where they spent the nights singing, dancing, and drinking; and that the defendant and his guests often disregarded the call for prayer during *Ramaḍān* (the month of Muslim fasting).[23] The residents added that they had asked the man to stop his activities or move out of the area, but he had refused. The *wālī* referred the case to the *qāḍī* for investigation. Several residents questioned by the *ᶜudūl* confirmed the charges. The *ᶜudūl* reported their findings to the *qāḍī*, but the accused was not available to answer charges.[24]

Sometimes the accused were arrested and sent to court for investigation. For example, police arrested a group of women on charges of suspicious behavior (possibly prostitution) and the governor of al-Bahnasā sent the women to the court for investigation.[25] The *qāḍī* consulted people who knew the women, discovered that they were respectable, and ordered their release.[26]

Whenever a suspicious-looking individual moved into a neighborhood, the residents would complain to the authorities and demand his eviction.[27] If the charges were proven, the individual was ordered to leave.[28]

In all of these cases, the report of the *ᶜudūl* was recorded in the registers for use when the defendant was arrested. For example, when a man was beaten and injured by someone who managed to escape, the brother of the victim rushed to court to demand investigation. The *ᶜudūl* did so,[29] and their report was the basis for the trial, which was conducted later, when the defendant was brought to court.[30] Similar action was taken when an employer reported to the court that one of his employees had been attacked and seriously injured by another employee.[31]

When the investigation was made at the *wālī*'s request, the results were reported to him. For example, when a *multazim* was killed by highway robbers, the *wālī* requested investigation.[32] The *ᶜudūl* and the *wālī*'s representative investigated the crime and questioned the peasants and other *multazims* of the area, who agreed that the raiders and other criminals hid in an area thickly planted with palm trees, and suggested that the trees be cut down. The report was sent to the governor for action.[33]

TRIALS

It was possible to conduct a civil trial in the absence of the defendant, but in criminal cases, both parties had to be present.

Trials were generally simple and mechanical. If the plaintiff failed to provide evidence against the defendant, as the *Sharī^cah* required, then the defendant could be required, upon the request of the plaintiff, to take a *yamīn* (oath) of his innocence. If the defendant admitted guilt, the trial was concluded and sentence delivered. These rules were generally applied in all trials with very little variation,[34] as the following will demonstrate.

• A woman charged that her brother had falsely accused her of fornication. The defendant admitted making the accusation, but claimed that he had gone to visit his sister and found her with a strange man. The defendant, however, failed to provide evidence for the truth of his allegation, while the woman provided a number of *shuhūd* to testify that she was a respectable woman and that her brother had met the man with whom she was accused in the street and not in her house. The brother was convicted.[35]

• A man voluntarily admitted fornication at a time when he was unmarried (the exact time was not mentioned) and demanded to be punished. The *qāḍī* proceeded to investigate the man's mental health by questioning people who knew him. The mental capacity of the defendant was also tested by asking him simple questions, such as what day, month, and year it was. Finally, the *qāḍī* gave the defendant a chance to reconsider his claims. When he persisted, he was sentenced.[36]

• Two men accused a Muslim convert of apostasy. The trial was conducted in the presence of a representative of the *wālī*. According to the plaintiffs, the defendant had been a Christian merchant who converted to Islam in Mecca and entered the mosque to pray in their presence. Later, however, he returned to Christianity and denounced Islam. The defendant admitted the charges but claimed that he had been forced to convert to Islam (no further explanation is given). The *qāḍī*, as the *Sharī^cah* required,[37] offered the defendant a chance to repent and return to Islam. When he accepted, he was given the two *shahādahs*, i.e., testifying that there is no god but God and that Muhammad is the Prophet of God, and was then released.

The following day the convert was brought to court on the same charge by the same individuals. Once more he was charged and admitted committing apostasy. The *qāḍī* decreed, in accordance with the *Sharīᶜah*, that the defendant be imprisoned for three days, during which time he was given a chance to repent each day. When he refused, he was convicted.[38]

Admission of guilt was rare. The defendant usually denied the charges and demanded that the plaintiff prove the evidence. The plaintiff usually had to provide only two *shuhūd*, but in cases of fornication the law required the testimony of four male *shuhūd*.[39] If the plaintiff provided the required *shuhūd* and the defendant did not challenge the testimony, the defendant was convicted.

• The plaintiff, an official appointed by the *wālī* on behalf of an heirless victim of murder, charged a member of the military with killing a free black man. The defendant denied the charges and demanded that the plaintiff provide evidence. Eight male *shuhūd* testified that they had seen the defendant kill the black man. The defendant did not challenge the testimony and was convicted.[40]

• Another plaintiff, whose status as *wakīl* pressing charges on behalf of his nephews was proved to the *qāḍī* through the testimony of two *shuhūd*, charged two men with killing his brother, the father of his clients, with a sword. He produced four male *shuhūd*, whose integrity was confirmed to the *qāḍī* through the testimony of the *ᶜudūl*. The defendants did not challenge the testimony and were convicted.[41]

• The plaintiff accused a janissary of beating him and produced two male *shuhūd* who testified that they saw the defendant hit the plaintiff in the face. The defendant did not challenge the testimony and was convicted.[42]

• A member of the military accused a *sharīf* (a person claiming descent from the family of the Prophet; pl. *ashrāf*) of striking him with a sword. Two male *shuhūd* from the military testified in support of his claim. The defendant was convicted.[43]

• The plaintiff accused the defendant of cursing him; two *shuhūd* testified in support of his allegations. The defendant was convicted.[44]

Occasionally a defendant did challenge the testimony of the *shuhūd*:

• An *amīr* (high-ranking military officer), accused two defendants, one of whom was absent, of murdering his slave.[45] The defendant present demanded evidence. The plaintiff produced four male *shuhūd* who testified that they had seen the defendants push the victim into a canal, where he drowned. The defendant charged that the *shuhūd* were poor people currently employed by the plaintiff and as such were obliged to testify in his favor to protect their own interests. The *qāḍī* disqualified the *shuhūd* for bias and dismissed the case, noting that if they actually had seen the crime committed, they could have called for help to stop the crime or to arrest the murderers. Nevertheless, the testimony was directed against the absent defendant.[46]

If the plaintiff failed to produce the requisite number of *shuhūd*, the case was dismissed:

• A woman accused a man of raping her.[47] The defendant demanded evidence. The woman left to bring evidence, but came back and declared that she had none. The case was dismissed.

• The head of the *ṭā'ifah* of milksellers, accusing a milkman of beating him,[48] was able to produce only one *shāhid*. He was then asked to produce a second *shāhid*, but at this point the *muṣliḥūn* intervened and made a *ṣulḥ* (settlement) between the two litigants, and the case was dropped.

In other cases where the plaintiff failed to provide evidence, he demanded that the defendant affirm his innocence under the *yamīn*. If the defendant took the *yamīn* the case was dismissed.

• A *sharīf* accused the attendant in a public bath, who was also a member of the military, of stealing money from his clothes. Since the plaintiff had no evidence, he requested that the defendant take a *yamīn* swearing to his innocence. Upon taking the *yamīn*, the defendant was declared innocent.[49]

The *ᶜudūl*'s report of investigation was sometimes decisive:

• When a man accused his next-door neighbor of stealing some of his personal effects from his house,[50] all the people questioned agreed that the defendant was an upright man and that he had no criminal record. The case was dismissed.[51]

In some cases, however, the defendant presented evidence that confirmed his innocence:

• A *sharīf* accused two Christians, one of whom was absent, of hitting him on his right eye and causing the loss of his eyesight. The defendant present denied the charges and claimed that the plaintiff had made the same allegations previously before the court of Bab al-Kharq and that the case had been dismissed. The plaintiff refused to acknowledge the defendant's *ḥujjah* issued by the court of Bab al-Kharq and demanded further evidence. The defendant produced two *ᶜudūl* who testified in support of the contents of the *ḥujjah*. The case was dismissed.[52]

• A woman accused her ex-husband of divorcing her suddenly, so that the resultant anguish led to the loss of her fetus. The defendant denied that his ex-wife had been pregnant at the time of divorce and produced four women *shuhūd* who testified that they saw the wife having her menstrual period five days before the divorce took place. The case was dismissed.[53]

The minimum number of *shuhūd* was generally maintained.[54] Cases of verbal assault and battery were dismissed if only one *shāhid* was presented. In cases of murder, the number of *shuhūd* was sometimes four, but at times was as high as eight. Women testified with men in civil cases[55] and some criminal cases such as battery.[56] But in other cases women only could testify (as in the one above). Cases which required the physical examination of women were referred to a woman appointed by the court. The integrity of the *shuhūd* was always confirmed to the *qāḍī* through the testimony of the *ᶜudūl*.

Theoretically, the *qāḍī* was supposed to hear the testimony of each *shāhid* separately.[57] The plaintiff was supposed to present the *shuhūd* within a certain undefined period of time, the registers stating only that the plaintiff requested time to bring his evidence and that he was granted "the legal period," and more.[58] Occasionally, it was stated that the plaintiff had requested three days, a week, or two weeks, to provide his evidence.[59]

The *yamīn* was administered only upon the request of the plaintiff to the defendant, in the hope that, out of fear of giving a false oath, he would admit his guilt.[60] Muslim defendants took the *yamīn* on the Qur'ān,[61] Christians on the Bible, and Jews on the Old Testament.[62]

SENTENCING

If the plaintiff could not provide evidence against the defendant the case was dismissed and the *qāḍī* ordered the plaintiff not to interfere with the defendant, who received a copy of the record to be used in case the plaintiff pressed the same charges against him in the future.[63]

According to Heyd, most criminal cases recorded in the registers of the courts of Anatolia in the fifteenth and sixteenth centuries mentioned no penalties. Often it was not even clear whether the defendant had been found guilty. The only function of the *qāḍī* there seems to have been to establish the facts.[64] This was not so in Ottoman Egypt, but a distinction must be made between those cases in which the defendant was not present (either because he escaped or because he simply refused to come) and those in which both parties were present. In the former the court simply investigated the case, established the facts, and made a report; but there was no trial until the defendant was brought to court,[65] and even then, as Heyd has rightly pointed out, generally not until the plaintiff was also present.[66] Occasionally, the plaintiff came alone and made formal charges against an absent defendant and requested a *ḥujjah* to that effect.[67] This was done simply to establish a criminal record for the offender, which could be used against him if he committed another crime. The Ottoman penal code decreed that, according to the principles of the *Sharīᶜah*, individuals with criminal records could be convicted if accused even if there was no evidence against them.[68]

But if both parties were present and the defendant was convited, the *qāḍī* always passed sentence, although the exact penalty is rarely detailed. The documents usually state that the convict was punished according to the *Sharīᶜah*,[69] and at times according to the *qānūn*.[70] In a few cases, the penalty was included: A murderer and an apostate were sentenced to death, a fornicator to one hundred lashes. Penalties for cases of *jarḥ* (personal injury) were often postponed until the fate of the victim was ascertained,[71] and the defendant imprisoned in the meantime.[72] In other cases of battery and verbal assault, those convicted might be chastised by beating, or simply chastised.[73] In not one case in the registers was someone found guilty without being sentenced. Nor is there any evidence that the *qāḍī* had to refer any cases to the sultan or to the *wālī* for confirmation of the sentence. Even in a murder case referred by the *wālī* in which a member of the military was sentenced to death, the *qāḍī*'s sentence was apparently final.[74]

Although according to Heyd the *ashrāf* were tried and punished only by the *naqīb al-ashrāf* (head of the people claiming descent from the family of the Prophet), and members of the *ṭawā'if* only by the *shaykhs* of the *ṭawā'if*,[75] this was not true in Egypt. Soldiers, *ashrāf*, and members of the *ṭawā'if* were brought to court for criminal offenses and, according to Raymond, the *ṣubāshī* in Egypt executed the penalties.[76] This seems to have been usually so, for the *ṣubāshī* was present in some trials, but in one case where a *sharīf* was sentenced to beating, it was stated that he was delivered to the *naqīb al-ashrāf* to receive the penalty.[77]

Finally, both Muslims and non-Muslims were tried in criminal cases before the court. Heyd's view that Jewish and Christian converts to Islam accused of committing apostasy were not tried by the ordinary law court[78] does not apply (see above, pp. 28-29).

Was the Ottoman penal code applied by the courts in Egypt in the seventeenth century? According to Heyd, it was largely disregarded at the time in many other parts of the empire--due, he thought, to the growing political influence of the religious scholars (ulema) and the *qāḍīs*, who never fully accepted the criminal regulations, particularly where they were contrary to the *Sharī^{c}ah*.[79] In Egypt, it is difficult to make an assessment because sentences are not mentioned in the registers. The few suggested are according to the *Sharī^{c}ah*, not the penal code. The letters appointing *qāḍīs* always stated that the *qāḍīs* must apply the *Sharī^{c}ah*, and do not mention the *qānūn*.[80] This should not be taken to mean that the *qānūn* was disregarded, for the penalties of the *qānūn* were to be applied instead of the *Sharī^{c}ah* penalty[81] in cases where the conditions of the *Sharī^{c}ah* could not be met.[82] The orders of the sultan did mention the *qānūn*,[83] and some documents stated that the defendant was punished in accordance with the *qānūn*.[84]

According to Heyd, Ottoman attempts to define the powers of the *wālīs*, military, and police were not successful. Executive officials tended to overstep the bounds of their authority and infringe on that of the *qāḍīs*. The rule of the *qānūn* that a criminal must not be punished unless he had been convicted by a *qāḍī* was largely disregarded. European observers claimed that the *qāḍī* dealt mainly with minor offenses while serious crimes were tried by the military governors and the police.[85]

This view is greatly overstated. It is clear from the cases already discussed that the *qāḍī* heard cases ranging from verbal assault to murder.[86] Cases could be brought not only by private individuals but also by the *wālī*, the provincial governors, and the police. Defendants might also be members of the military or the police.

• A man accused the *ṣūbāshī* of forcibly taking some of his personal effects. The *qāḍī* accepted the evidence and ordered the *ṣūbāshī* to return the items taken; he did.[87]

• A man complained to the *qāḍī* that the guard of the neighborhood where he lived was harassing him in an attempt to evict him. Other residents questioned agreed that the conduct of the defendant was normal. The *qāḍī* ordered the guard to leave the defendant alone.[88]

Finally (see below, pp. 62,67), soldiers who were also *multazim* were summoned and appeared in court to answer charges.

Nevertheless, some cases, criminal as well as civil, were submitted directly to the *wālī*, who did refer some of these to the court but others to the *Dīwān*.[89] The *qānūn* excluded from the jurisdiction of the *qāḍī* military crimes and crimes for which convictions could not be had because of lack of evidence according to the *Sharīᶜah*, and placed them under the jurisdiction of the *wālī* as the supreme representative of the sultan in Egypt.[90]

Occasionally, however, provincial governors and the *ṣūbāshī* did hear other cases and seem to have set punishments without a *qāḍī*'s decision. But those who lost then brought their cases to the *qāḍī* and demanded that the person who took them to the governor or the *ṣūbāshī* be punished or reimburse them:

• A man accused a husband and wife of enticing the *ṣūbāshī* to subject him to fines. The plaintiff produced several *shuhūd*, and the *qāḍī* decreed that the couple be punished.[91]

• When a plaintiff was able to produce evidence to the effect that he was taken to the *ṣūbāshī* and made to pay a fine without legal basis, the *qāḍī* ordered the defendant to pay back the fine in full. When the defendant refused, he was imprisoned.[92]

• Finally, another plaintiff accused a defendant of taking his son to the *ṣūbāshī*, where he was beaten and imprisoned illegally at the office of the governor of al-Gharbiyyah, and produced two *shuhūd*. The *qāḍī* ordered that the defendant be punished and imprisoned until the son of the plaintiff was returned.[93]

The *qāḍī* in seventeenth century Egypt thus had jurisdiction over all criminal cases involving both military and civilian litigants. Criminal cases were brought before the *qāḍī* by the *wālī*, the provincial governors, the *ṣūbāshī*, and private individuals. Except for the *wālī*, who was the supreme representative of the sultan with respect to cases involving military offenses and crimes which could not be prosecuted to conviction because of lack of evidence according to the *Sharīᶜah*, executive officials were not permitted to administer justice or to subject any individual to punishment without a *qāḍī*'s decision.

The law administered in court conformed to the *Sharīᶜah*, but since the latter stipulated penalties for only six crimes, the Ottomans introduced a penal code to supplement the *Sharīᶜah*, and there is evidence to indicate that the Ottoman penal code was enforced in Egypt during the seventeenth century.

Chapter VI
CIVIL CASES

Disputes related to sales, rentals, partnerships between people for the sharing of profit, hiring of animals or labor, and loans were heard before the courts.[1] The plaintiff was the person whose rights were allegedly violated, or his or her *wakīl*.[2] A *wakīl* bringing charges was always required to provide evidence of his status as agent, and usually did so through testimony by two *shuhūd*.[3] A woman could appoint another woman as her *wakīl*.[4] The plaintiff was responsible for bringing the defendant to court, but a trial could be held in absentia upon submission of proof that the defendant had refused to come or that his whereabouts had been unknown for an extended period.

Civil trials were conducted according to the same rules as criminal trials: First the plaintiff made charges against the defendant. If the defendant admitted the charges--as happened occasionally--he was ordered by the *qāḍī* to meet his obligations; if he refused, he was imprisoned, upon the request of the plaintiff:

• A *wakīl* acting for a wife charged the husband with failure to make payment on a loan. The defendant admitted taking out the loan, and the *qāḍī* ordered him to make payment. The two parties left and then returned to declare that all financial obligations between them were settled.[5]

• A butcher accused a defendant of failure to pay for meat. The defendant admitted the charges, but did not pay. The *qāḍī*, upon the request of the plaintiff, ordered the defendant imprisoned.[6]

In most cases, the defendant denied the charges and demanded that the plaintiff provide evidence:

• Plaintiff accused the defendant of refusing to pay for oranges sold and delivered to him. Two *shuhūd* testified in support of the plaintiff, and the *qāḍī* ordered the defendant to make payment. When he failed to do so, he was imprisoned, at the request of the plaintiff.[7]

• Plaintiff accused the defendant of failure to pay off a loan, and presented two *shuhūd* who testified in support of his claim. The *qāḍī* ordered the defendant to make payment, and the two parties departed.[8]

If the plaintiff provided only one *shāhid*, as when one man accused another of failure to make payment for wool sold and delivered to him, the case was dismissed.[9] (In that case plaintiff demanded the legally prescribed period to produce the second *shāhid*, but then returned and declared that he had no second *shāhid*.[10]) When a plaintiff had no evidence and demanded that the defendant affirm his innocence, if the defendant did so, he was declared innocent; but refusal was considered proof of guilt. Defendants could also ask plaintiffs to swear to the truth of their allegations.

• Plaintiff claimed that he gave his partner, a traveling merchant, money to buy coffee from Mecca, and accused his partner of failure either to buy the coffee or return the money. The plaintiff failed to provide evidence for his allegations and requested that the defendant take a *yamīn*. When the latter did so, the case was dismissed.[11]

• Plaintiff charged that defendant, his employee in a butcher shop, had collected money from sales but failed to turn it over to him, and requested that the defendant take the *yamīn*. When the latter refused, the *qāḍī* then asked the plaintiff to take the *yamīn* in support of his charges. When the plaintiff did, the *qāḍī* ordered the defendant to pay the amount specified. When he refused, he was imprisoned upon the request of the plaintiff.[12]

• Defendant admitted receiving a loan, but claimed to have made payment in full. The plaintiff denied receiving payment and requested evidence. The defendant failed to produce evidence and requested the *yamīn* from the plaintiff. When the plaintiff took the *yamīn*, the case was concluded, and the *qāḍī* ordered the defendant to make payment; when he refused, he was imprisoned.[13]

• An owner of a wheat mill accused a baker of failure to pay for wheat sold and delivered to him. The defendant admitted buying the wheat but claimed to have made payment in full. The plaintiff denied that he had been paid and requested evidence. The defendant requested the legally prescribed period to provide evidence, but returned and declared that he had no evidence. Since the defendant had not requested the *yamīn* of the plaintiff, his guilt was established. The *qāḍī* ordered the defendant to make payment; when he refused, he was imprisoned.[14]

In other cases, the defendant admitted the debt but claimed *iᶜsār* (insolvency). If the defendant supported his claim, usually through the testimony of two *shuhūd*, he was released from his obligations. If he did not, he had to make payment or face imprisonment.

• A *sharīf* accused two Jewish brothers of failing to repay a loan. The two defendants admitted receiving the loan, but claimed *iᶜsār* and produced several Muslim *shuhūd*, who testified before the *qāḍī* that the two defendants had lost all their possessions and that they did not own more than the garments they were wearing. The defendants were made to swear by God and His Prophet Moses that they were insolvent and that the testimony of the *shuhūd* was true. The defendants were released from their obligation.[15]

Those whose debts were far in excess of their income occasionally petitioned the *qāḍī* to set up an installment plan for them:

• A *multazim* with total debts of one million *niṣfs* and an annual net income of 125,000 *niṣfs*, petitioned the *wālī* for a payment plan through which he could pay his debts in installments. The *wālī* referred the case to the *qāḍī*, who decreed that he be allowed to pay his debts in eight annual installments amounting to 125,000 *niṣfs* each.[16] Unpaid taxes were to be paid before all other debts.[17]

A defendant sometimes admitted receiving a loan but pleaded that he had transferred his obligation from the plaintiff to a third party. In such cases, the defendant was required to provide evidence of a legally valid *ḥiwālah* (transfer of obligations). In order for the *ḥiwālah* to be legal and valid, it had to be agreed upon by the two parties and the two loans had to be identical in value and in kind (i.e., gold for gold, silver for silver, etc.). Moreover, the two debts must be payable at the same time. When a *ḥiwālah* took place, the creditor submitted his claims to the person to whom the obligation was transferred. If the latter refused to pay, he was sued.

• The transferee accused the person to whom a debt was transferred of failure to make payment on a loan.

The defendant admitted the charges but claimed *i^c^sār*. The plaintiff requested evidence, which the defendant failed to produce. The *qāḍī* then ordered the defendant to make payment.[18]

Where the loan was guaranteed, the plaintiff was entitled to press charges against the guarantor:

• A janissary claimed that he had loaned money to the son of the ex-consul of Venice with the guarantee of a Jewish translator working for the current Venetian consul, and that the debtor was insolvent. The plaintiff demanded that the guarantor pay the debt. The latter denied the charges and demanded evidence. The plaintiff produced two *^c^udūl* of the court which issued the deed of the debt to testify in support of his claims. The *qāḍī* ordered the defendant to meet his obligation. When he refused, he was imprisoned.[19]

If *rahīnah* (collateral) was supplied by a debtor or by a third party and the debtor failed to pay, the creditor could dispose of the collateral, with the permission of the *qāḍī:*

• The plaintiff claimed that he had made a loan to a man against a house owned by a third party, that the debtor was insolvent, and that the owner had refused to turn the house over to him or to come to court. This the plaintiff proved through the testimony of the *muḥḍir*, who had summoned the defendant several times but failed to bring him to court. The *qāḍī* authorized the creditor to dispose of the house.[20]

CASES REJECTED BY THE COURT

According to the *Sharī^c^ah* the production of alcohol is illegal.[21] Therefore, disputes related to transactions in alcoholic substances could not be heard in court.

• A Christian worker accused his employer, a janissary who was also engaged in the production of a beer-like beverage called *būzah*, of failure to pay him. The Ḥanbalī *nā'ib*, however, informed the plaintiff that disputes over obligations resulting from dealing with intoxicating or impure materials could not be heard.[22]

Some people would bring cases to the court of al-Bāb al-^c^Alī which had been heard previously in other courts. Upon presentation by the defendant of the document issued by the other court, the *qāḍī* dismissed the case.[23]

TRIALS IN ABSENTIA

In most cases, the plaintiff and the defendant were present at the trial. But if the plaintiff could prove to the *qāḍī* that the defendant had refused to come or that his whereabouts had been unknown for an extended period of time, a trial could be held in the absence of the defendant. That the defendant had refused to come was usually proved through the testimony of the *muḥḍir*.[24] If the defendant's whereabouts were unknown, the plaintiff was required to provide *shuhūd* who knew the defendant personally and could testify to that effect:

• The debtor had been absent for more than eight months and his creditor requested permission from the *qāḍī* to dispose of the debtor's personal belongings left behind as collateral.[25] Upon submission by the plaintiff of proof of the debtor's extended absence, the *qāḍī* granted authorization. *Ahl al-khibrah* were brought to the court to evaluate the worth of the personal belongings, and the appraised value minus the cost of searching for the defendant, was then applied against the debt.

Certain civil disputes also required the opinion of *ahl al-khibrah*:

• When a slave dealer was accused of selling a slave afflicted with leprosy, the *qāḍī* referred the slave to a member of the *ṭā'ifah* of the surgeons to be examined. The surgeon reported that the woman had a blackish wound in her vagina. The *qāḍī* decreed that the contract be abrogated and ordered the dealer to refund the agent the full price.[26]

CONTEMPT OF COURT

Almost all trials seem to have been orderly. In only one case was it hinted that the defendant had acted disrespectfully:

• Ironically, the defendant was himself a *qāḍī*.[27] He had borrowed money and failed to make payment, and the creditor complained to the *wālī*, who referred the case to the court. The *qāḍī* sent a *muḥḍir* to the defendant several times before he actually showed up in court. The trial then proceeded in the usual manner and the defendant admitted the charges and was asked to meet his obligations, but it seems that the defendant had first verbally and physically attacked the *muḥḍir*, though there are no details. The defendant was punished for his misconduct according to the *Sharīᶜah*. (Under the Ottoman penal code, officials appointed by an imperial *berāt* could only be chastised verbally.[28])

PENALTIES

If the charges were proved, the defendant was asked to meet his obligation. He was released if he did, and sometimes if he simply promised to do so. But if the defendant refused, the plaintiff could request that he be imprisoned. Defendants who served 100 days without being released by their creditors were automatically freed.[29] Some debtors were released by coming to terms with their creditors,[30] others by proving their *iᶜsār*,[31] and still others by making *kafālah* (bond).[32] The *kafīl* (guarantor) took the responsibility of bringing in the defendant when requested.[33]

Claims and counterclaims were often supported by *ḥujjahs*,[34] though the *ḥujjahs* themselves did not constitute evidence in court. If the other party refused to acknowledge the *ḥujjah*, the person presenting it had to prove its contents by the testimony of *shuhūd*.[35] Occasionally, however, when a *ḥujjah* originally issued in a provincial court was presented in a Cairene court, the *qāḍī* would ask the person presenting it to take an oath that its contents were valid.[36] But the *ḥujjahs* were merely records of binding transactions and did not give rise to legal obligations by themselves; they enabled those who wished to act counter to the *Sharīᶜah* to conform to the letter of the law while avoiding its spirit[37] through the use of cliches.[38] As a result, it is impossible to assess the degree to which transactions conformed to the *Sharīᶜah*.

Ribā (interest) is a case in point. The *Sharīᶜah* prohibited the payment of *ribā*,[39] while the Ottoman *qānūn* legalized it up to 10 per cent.[40] The loan contracts in the registers are silent on the subject.[41] A typical loan contract was recorded in the form of a declaration, as "A" declared that he had borrowed from or owed "B" a specific amount of money to be paid at a future date.[42] How much was principal and how much was interest was not specified.[43] Formula phrasing was used to conceal the substance of the transaction.

THE LEGAL STATUS OF NON-MUSLIMS *(ẔIMMĪS)*

Theoretically, the *Sharīᶜah* regulated the relations of non-Muslims with both individual Muslims and the Muslim state, but not the relation of non-Muslims with one another. Disputes between non-Muslims of the same community were heard by their own religious leaders.[44] A Muslim *qāḍī* could hear such disputes only if both litigants accepted his jurisdiction. The Ḥanafī school maintained that the *qāḍī* must try such cases if brought before him, but the Shāfiᶜī and Ḥanbalī schools maintained that he could decline to hear cases which were in contradiction with the *Sharīᶜah*.[45]

These principles were maintained in practice. Disputes between Muslims and non-Muslims were subject to the *Sharīᶜah* and were brought before the Muslim *qāḍī*, who also heard disputes between non-Muslims of different communities. In Egypt, for instance, there were two Jewish sects, the Rabbanites and the Karaites, who occasionally interfered in each other's religious affairs. In one such case two Karaite Jews complained to the *qāḍī* that two Rabbanite Jews had attacked and imprisoned them and kept them from celebrating their holy day. The plaintiffs submitted *fatwahs* issued by the four *muftīs* of Egypt stating that the two communities were separate and could not interfere in each other's affairs, and that those who did so should be punished. When the defendants denied the charges, the plaintiffs presented two Jewish and two Muslim *shuhūd* who testified in support of their claims, and the *qāḍī* ordered the defendants not to interfere in the affairs of the Karaite community.[46] Disputes between non-Muslims of the same community were also brought before the *qāḍī*, and the trial was also conducted according to the *Sharīᶜah* (see below, p. 44).

Non-Muslims had full property rights, including the right to buy slaves, and could establish their own *awqāf* for the maintenance of their religious institutions.[47]

This is not to say that non-Muslims were legally equal to Muslims. Theoretically, non-Muslim men could not marry Muslim women and could not testify against Muslims, though some jurists accepted such testimony where necessary, as in estate cases where the Muslim had died while traveling.[48]

Finally, if a Muslim killed or injured a non-Muslim, the *qiṣāṣ* (retaliation) penalty could not be applied[49]; instead, there was a lighter penalty of blood money or compensation. The principle of equality was usually applied according to the status of the victim, but the Mālikī school applied the principle to both aggressor and victim, i.e., if a non-Muslim killed a Muslim, the *qiṣāṣ* penalty could not be applied. The Mālikī, Shāfiʿī, and Ḥanbalī schools based the principle of equality on freedom and Islam. The Ḥanafī school based it on freedom and sex, so that *qiṣāṣ* could not be applied if a slave was killed by a free person or a woman by a man.[50]

Chapter VII

FAMILY LAW[1]

Litigation between husbands and wives centered around the financial obligations of the husband, which were treated like other kinds of debts. Most marriage contracts recorded in the registers made provision for the amount and method of payment of the *mahr* (dowry) the husband had to pay to the wife. Generally, the *mahr* was paid in part at the time of the contract (this portion was called *muqaddam al-ṣidāq*) and in part upon divorce or the death of the husband (*mu'akhkhar al-ṣidāq*). If the husband failed to pay the agreed *muqaddam*, the wife could deny him obedience and refuse to move to his house. But if the *muqaddam* was paid, the wife was required to obey her husband.[2]

• A Jew accused his Jewish wife of refusing to move to his house. The wife admitted the charges, but claimed that the husband had failed to pay the *muqaddam*. When the husband presented two Jewish *shuhūd* who testified that the wife had received the *muqaddam*, the *qāḍī* ordered the wife to move to her husband's domicile.[3]

• A divorced woman charged that her ex-husband had failed to pay the *mu'akhkhar al-ṣidāq*. The ex-husband denied the charges and presented a divorce decree issued by the court of Qūṣūn showing that the *wakīl* who had concluded the divorce on her behalf had released him from all his obligations to his wife. The woman, however, refused to acknowledge the decree and demanded further evidence. When the husband presented two *shuhūd* who testified to the validity of the contents of the decree, the charges were dismissed.[4]

If a woman could provide evidence that the husband had failed to meet his obligation, the *qāḍī* ordered the husband to pay. If the husband refused, he was imprisoned.[5] In one such case, the wife released her imprisoned husband from jail after he pledged to pay the *mu'akhkhar al-ṣidāq* in monthly installments. The agreement stated that if the husband failed to make one payment, the entire amount due would become payable at once.[6]

Most marriage contracts stipulated that the husband must maintain the wife and provide for her *kiswah* (clothing) at a level "equal to that of women of her status married to men of the husband's status,"[7] but others stipulated a specific monthly *kiswah* allowance to be paid to the wife.[8] It was also common for a wife to summon her husband to court after marriage and have him pledge to her before the *ᶜudūl* a specific amount for her *kiswah*.[9] These were probably cases where the husband was considering taking a second wife. If the husband was absent, the wife could petition the *qāḍī* to assign her an amount for her *kiswah* on behalf of her husband.[10] In all these cases, the wife was authorized to borrow the allowance from a third party if the husband was unable to pay, and demand that payment be made by the husband.[11] If the husband failed to pay, the wife could press charges against him:

• A wife accused her husband of failure to pay her the *kiswah*. The husband denied the charges but could not provide evidence. He then asked his wife to take an oath in support of her allegations. She did, the *qāḍī* asked the husband to pay, he refused, and upon the request of his wife, he was imprisoned.[12]

According to the *Sharīᶜah*, marriage could be terminated extrajudicially by mutual consent of both husband and wife or through the unilateral repudiation of the husband.[13] Husband and wife (occasionally represented by a *wakīl*) then came to court to have the divorce agreement notarized. The agreement usually provided for *mu'akhkhar al-ṣidāq*, the *nafaqah* (support) of the wife during the waiting period or during the time of pregnancy, and child support.[14] The wife sometimes released the husband from all his obligations, which suggests that she had initiated the divorce.[15] The husband sometimes made a commitment to meet his obligations,[16] but if he refused to do so, the wife could press charges against him.

• A woman charged that her husband had divorced her while she was pregnant, and that he had refused to pay *mu'akhkhar al-sidaq̄* and the *nafaqah*. The husband admitted the charges, paid the *mu'akhkhar al-ṣidāq*, and agreed to pay her one *niṣf* per day until she delivered the child.[17]

• A woman charged that her husband had divorced her and

demanded that he pay the *mu'akhkhar al-ṣidāq* and the accrued *kiswah*. The wife also claimed that she had asked the husband to pay *nafaqah* for their son, who was in her custody, but that he had refused. The husband presented a decree from the court of al-Ṣāliḥiyyah to the effect that he had divorced her at her own request and that she had released him from all his obligations. The wife demanded further evidence, the husband produced two *shuhūd* who testified to the validity of the decree, and the case was dismissed.[18]

The *nafaqah* agreed upon could be raised or reduced by the *qāḍī*, depending on the circumstances:

• A woman claimed that at the time of her divorce she had a male child and was also pregnant, and that her husband had agreed to pay two and one-half *niṣfs* daily as *nafaqah*. She asserted that such an amount was not enough for the support of her two children, but her husband had refused to increase the amount. The husband responded by claiming that he could not afford to pay more and he demanded custody of his son. The *qāḍī* refused to grant custody of the child to his father so long as the mother was unmarried, and ordered the husband to increase the *nafaqah* by two *niṣfs* per day.[19]

The husband, too, could petition the *qāḍī* to reduce the amount of *nafaqah* if he was unable to pay it:

• A man agreed at the time of divorce to pay his wife five *niṣfs* per day as *nafaqah*. Later he submitted an affidavit to the Ḥanafī *muftī* stating that his total income was four *niṣfs* per day, and he was unable to pay. The *muftī* issued a *fatwah* stating that the amount of the *nafaqah* should be determined by the actual means of the husband, regardless of the amount agreed upon at the time of divorce.[20] The man submitted the *fatwah* to the *qāḍī*, who reduced the *nafaqah* to two *niṣfs* per day.

DIVORCE BY JUDICIAL DECREE

According to all Muslim schools of law, the wife could obtain a divorce only by judicial decree.[21] The Ḥanafī school recognized impotence of the husband as the only valid ground, but the other schools recognized desertion, failure to support the wife, cruelty, and incurable disease as equally valid grounds.[22] Marriage contracts found in the registers often included terms which, if not fulfilled by the husband, allowed the wife to obtain a divorce. Such terms included failure to provide for the wife's *kiswah*, beating the wife, marrying a second wife, taking a concubine, moving the wife from the place specified in the contract, or forcing her to live with others.[23] The Ḥanafī school would not uphold terms which contradicted the principles of Ḥanafī law, such as marrying a second wife,[24] but the Ḥanbalī school enforced all of these provisions.[25] This explains why all cases of divorce initiated by wives were handled by the Ḥanbalī *nā'ib*, with the permission of the *qāḍī ᶜaskar*, although the Ḥanbalī school had very little following in Egypt.

• With the permission of the *qā'im makām*, the Ḥanbalī *nā'ib* heard three male *shuhūd* (confirmed by two *ᶜudūl*) testify that they knew the woman, Tighar, and her husband, ᶜAlī, and that after the marriage was consummated, the husband left the country for an entire year, leaving his wife without support or knowledge of his whereabouts. The *shuhūd* also testified that the woman had no one from whom to borrow money, and that her husband had left no property, money, or relatives who might support her. The woman then took a *yamīn* to the effect that the testimony of the *shuhūd* was correct. The *nā'ib* granted her request for divorce.[26]

INHERITANCE

The two courts of al-Qismah al-ᶜAskariyyah and al-Qismah al-ᶜArabiyyah supervised allocation of inheritances.[27] The former handled property left by soldiers, officers, bureaucrats, ulema, and *ashrāf*,[28] the latter that left by Muslim and non-Muslim peasants, artisans, and merchants.[29]

According to Ottoman *qānūn*, when anyone died the treasury had to be notified immediately.[30] A representative of the treasury was sent to the home of the deceased to determine whether the state had any rights over the inheritance (as happened when the deceased left no heirs or if the shares of the heirs did not exhaust the property).[31] The main function of the treasury representative at first was to check the legitimacy of the heirs. This was occasionally a subject of dispute.

• A woman claimed that she and three male cousins had survived her father, but that the representative of the treasury had prevented them from acquiring their legal shares. The representative of the treasury admitted the charges but demanded evidence to the effect that the deceased was survived by three cousins. At a later date the representative of the treasury declared that he had heard the required evidence (possibly through the testimony of *shuhūd*) and dropped all the treasury's claims.[32]

The treasury referred cases in which the state had rights to the *qassām* for division,[33] and legal heirs also referred other cases to the *qassām*.[34] A committee was then formed, under the supervision of the *qassām*, to survey the estate. The committee was made up of the legal heirs,[35] the representative of the treasury when appropriate, *ᶜudūl* from the court,[36] and *ahl al-khibrah*, whose services were needed for the evaluation or sale of properties.[37] Female heirs participated in their own behalf or appointed a *wakīl*. Minor heirs were represented by a *waṣī* (guardian) appointed by the *qāḍī*.[38] The *ahl al-khibrah* had to be familiar with the particular properties evaluated or sold. For example, when the deceased was a mutton butcher, the *shaykh* of the *ṭā'ifah* of mutton butchers evaluated the stock of mutton left by the deceased.[39] When the deceased was a copper merchant, a copper merchant supervised the sale of the inventory,[40] which was sold in different Cairo markets over an extended period to avoid causing a drop in the price.[41]

The committee began by making a survey of the decedent's estate: personal belongings, commodities and equipment, urban properties, loans outstanding, animals, and slaves. Each asset was valued, and debts and expenses were listed. These included the cost of burying the deceased in a fashion worthy of him, *mu'akhkhar al-ṣidāq* due to the widow, the cost of estate administration, and debts owed to the state (unpaid taxes) and to creditors. The balance was then divided among the legal heirs according to the *Sharīᶜah*.[42]

Disputes over inheritance centered around moneys borrowed or property sold by the deceased before his death:

• A man claimed that he had lent another man 15,000 *niṣfs* before his death, but that the heirs were refusing to acknowledge the debt. The heirs denied the charges and demanded additional evidence. The reliability of the plaintiff's two *shuhūd* was confirmed not only through the testimony of two *ᶜudūl* but also by the *qāḍī*'s investigation of them "privately and publicly," presumably by interviewing individuals who knew them. Finally, the plaintiff was also asked to take a *yamīn* in support of his claims. The *qāḍī* then ordered the heirs to pay off the loan.[43]

• A man claimed that he had inherited a house from his deceased father, but that the occupant refused to turn it over to him. The defendant occupant admitted the charges, but claimed that he had bought the house from the father before his death. The plaintiff refused to acknowledge the defendant's *ḥujjah* and demanded further evidence. The two *ᶜudūl* who had witnessed the *ḥujjah* testified to its contents, and the case was dismissed.[44]

THE STATE AND INHERITANCE

Although Gibb and Bowen have claimed that the Ottoman government confiscated the property of decedents belonging to the ruling class whether or not they were survived by heirs,[45] the records demonstrate the contrary. If a merchant or an artisan died and was succeeded only by a wife and a daughter, the wife received one-eighth, the daughter one-half, and the treasury the balance.[46] A widower inherited half his wife's estate, and the other half went to the treasury.[47] The situation was the same for members of the military or the bureaucracy: A deceased *amīr* was survived only by his wife, who received one-fourth of his estate, with the balance going to the treasury.[48] But when a deceased military officer was survived by one or more wives and a daughter or daughters,[49] or by a mother and a brother,[50] the treasury received nothing.

If there had been tax evasion, the *wālī* ordered the treasury to seize the property and sell it.[51] Occasionally, the court heard disputes with regard to manumitted slaves who had formerly belonged to the person whose property was confiscated. The person claiming to be free was, in such cases, released if *shuhūd* could testify to his manumission.[52]

If the state was to share in property left by individuals not belonging to the military or the bureaucracy, the first 10,000 *niṣfs* went to the *bayt al-māl al-ᶜāmmah* (public treasury), and anything in excess of that went to the *bayt al-māl al-khāṣṣah* (private treasury of the sultan),[53] which also received all the state's inheritance from members of the military or the bureaucracy.[54]

THE LEGAL STATUS OF WOMEN[55]

Arab women, it has been claimed, were dominated by their fathers, brothers, and husbands, and played no role in the economic life of the society.[56] The records show a somewhat different picture. In Egypt under the Ottomans, women of age came to court to press charges on their own behalf or to answer charges made against them.[57] Although some women appointed *wakīls* to act for them, the *wakīl* was sometimes another woman.[58] Women also testified along with men in both criminal and civil cases, and testified alone in cases involving pregnancy and the examination of other women (though it took the testimony of two women to equal that of one man). Women were also appointed by the court as *nāẓirs* of *awqāf*,[59] and *waṣīs* over minors.[60]

Minor women were given in marriage by their fathers.[61] Women of age married of their own free will, with the father or a brother acting as a *wakīl*,[62] or sometimes without the intervention of a *wakīl*.[63] Women could pursue their rights against their husbands in court. Women of age were as free as men to dispose of their property through sale[64] and *waqf*.[65] The property of a wife was separate from that of her husband, and both spouses were allowed to dispose of up to one-third of their property through a will.[66] Women's economic activities, however, were mostly centered around buying, selling, and renting urban properties.[67]

Chapter VIII

THE ROLE OF THE COURT IN URBAN ADMINISTRATION

The court had a definite role to play in enforcing building regulations, the social and religious rights of individuals and groups, market regulations, the laws of the *ṭawā'if*, and taxation.

THE POPULATION

The common division of the Egyptian population into a tax-exempt, non-productive, and politically active ruling class (the military, bureaucrats, and the ulema), and a taxpaying, productive, but politically passive subject class (merchants, artisans, and peasants) is an over-simplification.[1] Many high-ranking military officers were *multazims*, and acquired large quantities of grain and animals (taxes were paid partly in cash and partly in kind). When they eventually traded in these commodities,[2] they were taxed despite their military status.[3] On the other hand, it was not uncommon to find merchants and peasants exempted from taxes as an inducement to expand production or commercial activities. For example, by order of the Sultan in 1082 A.H./1671 A.D., Maghrebī (North African) merchants who imported coffee and spices from Arabia during the annual pilgrimage were exempted from customs duties.[4] In 1050 A.H./1640 A.D., some peasants were exempted from taxes in return for maintaining and guarding an irrigation canal.[5] A year later, peasants were partly exempted from taxes to encourage them to settle in a certain uncultivated area.[6] Finally, as will become obvious, the merchants, artisans, and peasants were not as "passive" as is generally believed.

PHYSICAL ORGANIZATION

The urban centers of Egypt were made up of small residential areas called *ḥārahs* (neighborhoods), each with a few small shops and public facilities like a mosque, school, church or synagogue, public baths, or a water fountain.[7] Each *ḥārah* comprised a number of streets and alleys connected by a main road and surrounded by a wall with a gate. Regulations regarding buildings and changes in their structure or the structure of the *ḥārah* which in pre-Ottoman times had been enforced by the *muḥtasib* were in the seventeenth century enforced by the court, with the assistance of building inspectors.[8] When a new house or an addition to an existing house was built, the owner requested that the *ᶜudūl* be sent to confirm that the building complied with the building code. In one such case, the *ᶜudūl* and the inspector reported that the building was in full compliance: "A mounted warrior or a loaded camel can pass through the main street in which the building is located, unhampered. Moreover, the building does not infringe on its neighbors' rights to light, air, and scenery."[9]

Occasionally it was claimed that new doors on old houses infringed on the rights of neighbors to privacy, which was an important right, or threatened the security of the area. One man complained that a new door on a house across the street had caused the area in front of his house to become a gathering place for "evil people." Upon confirmation of the charges by the *ᶜudūl*, who questioned the neighbors, the defendant was asked to remove the new door and to block the opening with stone and cement.[10] Owners of vacant lots in the neighborhood were occasionally ordered by the court, upon complaint by neighbors, to fence their land to keep it from becoming a refuge for undesirables.[11]

Considerations of privacy occasionally required court-supervised adjustments in the geography of the *ḥarah*:

• A group of Muslims and non-Muslims living on adjacent streets in a single *ḥārah* complained that people on the street could see their naked women inside the public bath on their way to the dressing rooms. They requested that the *ᶜudūl* and the inspector examine the place and make recommendations for adjustments. The inspector suggested blocking one road and opening a new one, and the changes were accepted by the two communities.[12]

Occasionally disputes arose from changes in the functions of buildings, or from changes which threatened the safety of a building:

• A man complained that his neighbor who operated one grist mill next door had recently begun to operate a second one, thus causing his house to shake. The inspector and the *ᶜudūl* examined the building while the two grist mills were in operation and confirmed the charges. The neighbors stated that the second mill had always been there, but had been put out of service thirty years before on the grounds of security, and that the owner of the mill had only recently begun operating it. The *qāḍī* ordered the owner to stop using the second mill.[13]

• Another man claimed that he owned a place which he intended to turn into a sewing shop, but that the woman next door was preventing him from doing so. The woman claimed that the noise from the shop would disturb her. The *ᶜudūl* found that the woman's house was separated from the place intended for a sewing shop by a wide street and thus her objection was unfounded. The people of the *ḥārah* agreed that such a shop was good for the community. The *qāḍī* ordered the woman not to interfere with the project.[14]

• A man complained that an endowed house next door to his own was in a state of ruin and, as such, posed a threat to his house as well as others. He demanded that the *nāẓir* of the *waqf* be ordered to repair the house to prevent damage to the neighborhood.[15] Examination of the six-story building by the *ᶜudūl* and the inspector revealed a crack in the structure, some stories without doors, and the absence of a roof. The lower stories were built of brick, but the sixth was wood and bamboo. The neighbors were concerned that the house would collapse and that the wood and bamboo would again catch fire, as it had in the past, though the fire had been put out before it spread. The people of the *ḥārah* requested that the building be rented and that the rent be used for restoration. The *ᶜudūl* and the inspector reported their findings to the *qāḍī* for action.

In similar cases, the court usually appointed a new *nāẓir* for the *waqf* and demanded that he repair the building using the revenues of the *waqf*.

Urban properties were owned privately or belonged to *awqāf*. Privately-owned properties were rented directly by their owners, but properties which belonged to *awqāf* were rented by the *nāẓirs*, usually for three years, but sometimes for as long as ninety years.[16] If the property was part of a *waqf*, the *qāḍī ᶜaskar* had to approve the rental agreement.[17] The rent was usually determined according to the standard market rental value of similar properties, estimated by a member of the *ṭā'ifah* of the builders. Rental agreements extending over a period of ninety years usually stated that the property was rented for thirty consecutive contracts of three years each, with specific rent and distinctive wording for each contract, and that each contract was separate from the preceding and the succeeding one. Such agreements occasionally gave rise to disputes.[18]

• Three tenants complained that they had rented *waqf* houses in 1010 A.H./1601 A.D. for a period of ninety years, at an annual rent at the time of 120 *niṣfs*. Later the property was released from the *waqf* by the defendant landlord, who had given the *waqf* another place. The landowner had raised the rent gradually until it had reached 9,000 *niṣfs* for the three houses annually. The plaintiffs claimed that they were poor and could not pay the rent, and submitted an estimate made by members of the *ṭā'ifah* of the builders showing that the current rents for equivalent properties in the area were 500 *niṣfs*, 900 *niṣfs*, and 1,000 *niṣfs* for the three houses. The *qāḍī* ruled that the estimates submitted were reasonable and must be accepted by the landlord.[19]

Disputes centered around non-payment of rents were handled by the court like other debts and obligations.

SOCIAL ORGANIZATION

The *ḥarahs* were usually homogeneous by nationality, religion, or occupation. For example, Ḥārat al-Maghāribah was inhabited mostly by North Africans, Ḥārat al-Naṣārā by Christians, Ḥārat al-Yahūd by Jews, Ḥārat al-Naḥḥāsīn by copper merchants, and Ḥārat al-Khayyāmiyyah by tentmakers.[20] Members of the military tended to concentrate; twenty *amīrs* from various regiments lived on the same street.[21]

Each *ḥārah* was headed by a *shaykh* who represented the community to the authorities. The *ḥārah* inhabited by members of the same craft or trade was headed by the *shaykh* of the *ṭā'ifah* of the craft. Non-Muslim *ḥarahs* were headed by their religious leaders.

The internal homogeneity of the *ḥārah* and the fact that it was responsible for its own security and taxation tended to create a community spirit and collective action in maintaining standards of morality, security, and public services.

Residents sometimes complained that suspicious-looking people were threatening the security of the *ḥārah*:

• Residents of a *ḥārah* complained to the *wālī* that a neighbor had entertained a suspicious-looking individual in his home and demanded that the host be evicted to prevent his guest from returning. The case was referred to the court for action.[22]

Individuals who conducted themselves "disrespectfully" could also be evicted at the request of the community:

• The people of one *ḥārah* complained to the *wālī* that three women had a habit of swearing, cursing, and beating their neighbors, and demanded that the women be evicted.[23] (The fact that these women were all single may have had something to do with the request; in certain *ḥārahs* single people were not welcomed.[24]) The case was referred to the court and upon confirmation of the charges, the women were made to move out of the area.[25] Those who were accused of drinking alcohol,[26] or gossiping about the people in the *ḥārah*[27] could also be ordered to move.

Most of the community services, like baths, water fountains, and mosques, were maintained by *awqāf* established by sultans, *wālīs*, bureaucrats, merchants, and artisans, and were closely supervised by the court:

• The people of one *ḥārah* complained to the *wālī* that the *nāẓir* of the *waqf* which supported the public baths for men and women in the area had rented both baths to a man who neglected them to the point that they went out of service. The people asked that the baths be rented to a man they had chosen because of his good conduct, on condition that he revive and keep them in service. The *wālī* referred the matter to the *qāḍī* to carry out the will of the people. The man chosen had to sign a three-year contract for the baths, with the stipulation that he would put them back in order.[28]

• Residents complained to the *wālī* that the mosque in their *ḥārah* was neglected, and demanded an investigation. The *wālī* referred the case to the court. The investigation confirmed the allegations of the community. The *nāẓir* was fired, and a new *nāẓir* was appointed (with the consent of the community), on the condition that he would use the revenue of the *waqf* to repair and maintain the mosque.[29]

The registers do not state how many individuals took part in these cases. Usually a few people were named and the rest were referred to as the "others"[30] or as *al-jam^{c} al-ghafīr* (large crowd).[31] The number of those named ranged between seven and twenty-one,[32] and usually included soldiers, bureaucrats, merchants, and artisans.[33] Sometimes the complainant was simply "*ahl al-ḥārah*" (the community), with no one named.[34]

The ethnic, religious, or occupational homogeneity of the *ḥārah* did not mean that people lived in social isolation. Merchants and artisans lived side by side with soldiers and bureaucrats.[35] Many soldiers and bureaucrats were also engaged in industry or in trade. Despite a tendency toward grouping in certain areas, non-Muslims sometimes lived among Muslims or in adjacent streets, and interacted in public places like the public baths,[36] and in the Muslims courts of law inside the mosques.[37] It was not uncommon to find Muslims defending a non-Muslim against another Muslim,[38] or to find a non-Muslim bailing a Muslim out of jail,[39] or to find a Muslim man marrying a non-Muslim woman, without the wife changing her religion.[40]

The most impressive interaction between the two communities occurred in business, where there were numerous exchanges in commodities, urban properties, and loans between Muslims and non-Muslims.[41] Muslims frequently appointed non-Muslims as *wakīls* in financial affairs.[42] Jews and Christians were also appointed as *multazims*.[43] The *ṭawā'if* of merchants and artisans were at times co-religious, though some were made up only of Jews. Finally, although the relationships between non-Muslims of the same community were outside the scope of the *Sharī^{c}ah*, non-Muslims often brought their disputes before the *qāḍī* and demanded that the *Sharī^{c}ah* be applied.

This is not to say that the two communities were legally or socially equal, nor to suggest that complete social harmony prevailed.[44] The *wālī* ordered non-Muslims not to ride horses or to wear fezzes, and in public baths they were to wear red or black thread necklaces or display their religious symbols, such as the cross in the case of Christians (both violators and the bath attendant could be punished[45]). Finally, non-Muslims could not build churches, monasteries, or temples above the level of the nearby Muslim places of worship, although higher buildings already existing could stand:

• A Muslim complained to the court that the Christians in his neighborhood had recently added new buildings to their monastery, thus causing it to be above the level of the Muslim places around it. The other Muslims in the *ḥārah*, who were apparently less fanatical than the plaintiff, told the *ᶜudūl* that no additions had been made to the monastery for thirty years. The case was dropped.[46]

The *Sharīᶜah* allowed non-Muslims to practice their beliefs freely, and required the government to prevent Muslims as well as other non-Muslims from intervening in their affairs. Occasionally, hostilities aroused by religious fanaticism were brought before the *qāḍī*:

• A group of Jews claimed that for many years their funeral processions had passed along a main road which cut across a Muslim residential area and a Muslim cemetery. Lately, a Muslim had been trying to force them to use another road, which they felt was unsafe, on the grounds that their passage through the main road was harmful to the Muslim community. Further explanation was not given. The Jews presented *fatwās* issued by the four *muftīs*, orders from six *wālīs*, and a petition signed by forty-nine ulema, all to the effect that non-Muslims had the right to use Muslim roads day and night and that no one should prevent them from doing so. The *qāḍī* ordered the Muslim defendant to stop interfering in the affairs of the Jews.[47]

Another example of the hostilities between the two communities is the accusation of apostasy made by Muslims against Muslim converts.[48] In one documented case, the plaintiffs and the defendant were all merchants who traveled to the Muslim holy cities of Arabia for trading, and professional jealousy may have caused the complaint.

Muslim Sufi groups also tried occasionally to intervene in each other's affairs:

• The *shaykh* of the Aḥmadiyyah Sufi brotherhood complained that the *shaykh* of the Rifāᶜiyyah brotherhood was interfering in their affairs. The *qāḍī* ordered the accused *shaykh* to stop, and also ordered a public announcement to that effect.[49]

ECONOMIC ORGANIZATION[50]

If the *ḥārah* was the unit of social organization in the city, the *ṭā'ifah* was the unit of economic organization. All persons engaged in the production of goods and services were organized in *ṭawā'if*. Although their number is impossible to determine,[51] the *ṭawā'if* of the merchants included those for dealers in grains, copper, textiles, silk, spices, slaves, jewels, vegetables, fruits, and mutton. The *ṭawā'if* of the artisans embraced the manufacture of sugar, wax, oil, sweets, fruit drinks, carpets, blankets, shoes, and cloth, and there were also *ṭawā'if* for surgeons, barbers, tailors, butchers, water carriers, porters, donkey, camel, and horse drivers, builders, and coffee shop and public bath owners.[52] How many members each *ṭā'ifah* had is also impossible to determine from the information available. Whenever a *ṭā'ifah* brought a dispute before the court, some names were mentioned, and the rest were referred to as the "others." Those named were usually among the hierarchy of the *ṭā'ifah*, like the *shaykhs* and *usṭahs* (masters).

Members of each *ṭā'ifah* lived in all parts of the city (Cairo, old Cairo, and Būlāq),[53] though sometimes members of a particular *ṭā'ifah* were concentrated in a single quarter.[54] The *ṭā'ifah* of the jewelers included Muslims and Christians,[55] the *ṭā'ifah* of the merchants of textiles and spices included Muslims and Jews, but Jewish butchers, for perhaps obvious reasons, were organized in a *ṭā'ifah* separate from Muslim butchers.[56]

At the head of each *ṭā'ifah* stood the *shaykh*. Below him came the *naqīb* (lieutenant), then the *usṭahs*, and, finally, the *ṣanayᶜīs* (journeymen) and the *ṣabīs* (apprentices). Some *ṭawā'if*, like the linen merchants, had two *shaykhs*,[57] and sometimes one *shaykh* headed more than one *ṭā'ifah*, like the man who headed the *ṭawā'if* of the camel, the horse, and the donkey drivers, or the one who headed those of the sweets-makers and the punch-makers.[58]

The *usṭahs* of the *ṭā'ifah* elected the *shaykh* from among themselves. They then proceeded to the court to seek confirmation of the new *shaykh*, and a *ḥujjah* to that effect was issued:

• *Usṭahs* from the *ṭā'ifah* of the bone-bracelet-makers declared before the *qāḍī* that they had chosen al-Ḥājj Mūsā as their *shaykh* on the condition that he would distribute the materials needed for production among members of the *ṭā'ifah* according to the *qānūn* and to custom, and that he would give no member preference over the others in the distribution. The party then requested that the *qāḍī* recognize and confirm Mūsā. Confirmation was granted and a record was issued. After that, Shaykh Mūsā appointed Aḥmad Abū al-Naṣr, with the consent of the members, as *naqīb* of the *ṭā'ifah*.[59]

• The *shaykh*, the former *shaykh*, and a number of *usṭahs* of the *ṭā'ifah* of the dyers in blue declared that they had chosen Muḥammad b. Nūr al-Dīn as *shaykh* of their *tā'ifah* on the basis of his good and religious conduct and his knowledge of the regulations and the methods of their craft. The elected *shaykh* promised to uphold the customs and the laws of the *ṭā'ifah* as had his predecessors, to distribute the indigo justly among the members, and not to subject any members to injustice. The *qāḍī* confirmed him on that basis and a document was issued to that effect.[60]

The *shaykh* was generally elected on the basis of his personal character (i.e., good conduct, honesty, and religious behavior) and his knowledge of the *qānūns* of the craft. His responsibilities were to distribute raw materials and labor among the members, enforce the guild *qānūn*, settle disputes between the members, collect taxes, and negotiate prices of goods and services with the *muḥtasib*.

The *shaykh* was elected for an unlimited term. A new *shaykh* was appointed when his predecessor died,[61] or was discharged by the *usṭahs* for refusal or neglect to arbitrate or settle disputes or injustices committed against, or mistreatment of, the members:

• Al-Ḥājj Muḥammad b. Nuṣayr and seventy-one *usṭahs* (mentioned by name) and others complained to the *qāḍī* that Khalīl, the *shaykh* of their *ṭā'ifah*, the blanket makers, was evil and corrupt and that he beat the members and confiscated their money. The members requested that Khalīl be discharged and that Muḥammad b. Nuṣayr be installed as a *shaykh* because he was honest, pious, knowledgeable in the *qānūns* and customs of the craft, and merciful. The *qāḍī* discharged Khalīl and installed Muḥammad as the new *shaykh*.[62]

• Al-Ḥājj Abū al-Naṣr and fourteen members of the *ṭā'ifah* of the merchants of fat requested that their *shaykh* be discharged because he had violated the *qānūn* and that al-Ḥājj Abū al-Naṣr be installed as his replacement. The *qāḍī* discharged the current *shaykh* and installed Abū al-Naṣr.[63]

• Members of the *ṭa'ifah* of the oil-pressers complained to the *wālī* about the *shaykh*. The *wālī* referred the case to the *qāḍī*, requesting confirmation of the new *shaykh* to be chosen by the members. Accordingly, eighty-one members of the *ṭā'ifah* and the *muḥtasib* agreed on a new *shaykh*. After confirmation by the court, the new *shaykh* promised to respect the powerful among the members and to be merciful toward the weak and the poor; to follow the rules of custom; and to deliver to the members the five and one-third *ardabbs* of sesame at the rate of seventy *niṣfs*.[64]

How many members participated in the election or discharge of the *shaykh* cannot be determined precisely. The number of individuals named in the registers ranged from fourteen to eighty-one, most of them *usṭahs*.[65]

Occasionally, the elected *shaykh* appointed a *wakīl* as acting *shaykh*, though only with the consent of the members.[66] The *shaykh* was sometimes elected before the *wālī*, who then requested that the *qāḍī* recognize and confirm him.[67]

The *naqīb* was appointed by the *shaykh* as his assistant, with the consent of the members.[68] Though most *ṭawā'if* had one *naqīb*, the *ṭā'ifah* of the Jewish butchers, among others, had three: one in Ḥārat al-Yahūd, one in Ḥārat Bāb al-Shaᶜriyyah, and one in Ḥārat al-Madābigh.[69]

The functions of the *naqīb* overlapped those of the *shaykh*. He at times represented the *ṭā'ifah* in disputes between members as well as in pricing and tax negotiations with the representatives of government, like the *muḥtasib* and *multazim*.

Upon joining the *ṭā'ifah*, a new member was attached to one of the *usṭahs*, who taught him the craft. After the training period, the *ṣabī* became a *ṣanayᶜī* (for how long is not clear from the documents), then an *usṭah*,[70] at which point he went into business for himself.[71]

The rules of some *ṭawā'if* limited the number of members. The *ṭā'ifah* of the slave-dealers had only twelve members, all of whom had to be sons of slave-dealers.[72] The *qānūns* might also set other limits: Each jeweler, for instance, was allowed only three workers in his shop, and could not raid the workers of other jewelers.[73] Blanket-dyers could have no more than seven vats for dying.[74] Fruit-juice makers had to use pure sugar, and raw sugar was prohibited.[75] The *shaykh* of the oil-pressers could charge only seventy *niṣfs* for every five and one-third *ardabbs* of sesame.[76] Builders could not erect a building without the *shaykh*'s permission, and any builder who committed errors in building was prevented from practicing. Builders or brick-layers had to be paid six *niṣfs* for every day of work from sunrise to sunset; hod-carriers were to earn three *niṣfs* per day, and minors one and one-half *niṣfs* per day.[77]

In all the *ṭawā'if* the *shaykh* had the responsibility of allocating materials among the members according to their capacity.[78] Non-members could buy materials from the *shaykh* only after the requirements of members were met.[79] Members could not try to monopolize materials or labor,[80] or try to take the customers of other members, or try to sell their products outside their shops or markets, or send their employees door to door.[81]

To control the quality, prices, and fair distribution among members of the *ṭawā'if* there were *sūqs* (central markets) and *wakālahs* (bazaars) for the main items of industry and trade. The *wakālah* of Muṣṭafā Aghā in Būlāq was the center for all agricultural products coming to Cairo from Lower and Upper Egypt (including cheese, oil, shortening, honey, cotton, fruits, and leather).[82] The sultans instructed the *wālīs* and the *qāḍī* ᶜ*askars* that none of these products should be sold outside this market and that the *muḥtasib* and the *ṣubashī* were to enforce this rule.[83] Another *wakālah* in Bāb al-Shaᶜriyyah, known as the *waqf* of Shaykh ᶜAbd al-Qādir al-Dashṭūshī, was the center for selling geese, chickens, and eggs coming from the countryside.[84] Other *sūqs* specialized in goods imported from India, Arabia, and the Sudan, like spices, coffee, and slaves.[85] Each *sūq* or *wakālah* had a staff of guards and weighers, a customs officer, and a *multazim*.[86]

These strict regulations protected the members' economic interests by preventing monopolies of materials and labor, or changes in methods of production. They were also in harmony with the state's obligation to maintain social and economic order by stabilizing prices and securing the flow of goods, and by protecting the society against unfair business practices like fraud in weights and measures, inferior quality of goods, and price-gouging.[87] The state therefore supported the rules of the *ṭawā'if* and enforced them through the *qāḍī* and the *muḥtasib*. Prices were negotiated in court between the *muḥtasib* and the *shaykhs* or the *naqībs* of the various *ṭawā'if*. For example, the *naqībs* of the Jewish butchers in Cairo agreed before the *qāḍī* that they would charge Jews one *niṣf* per pound above the price fixed for meat sold to Muslims.[88] The extra *niṣf* was apparently for preparing the meat in accordance with the Jewish dietary laws. Lists of prices fixed by the *muḥtasib* and the *shaykhs* were regularly sent to the court.[89] Although generally the *muḥtasib* toured the market to enforce the rules concerning weights, measures, quality, and prices,[90] by order of the *wālī* the weight units used by the sugar merchants were supposed to be checked by the *qāḍī*, not the *muḥtasib*.[91] Members of the *ṭā'ifah* who violated the regulations were brought before the *qāḍī*:

• In the presence of the *muḥtasib* and the *shaykh* of the *ṭā'ifah* of the candlemakers, the plaintiff complained that the *shaykh* had accused him before the *muḥtasib* of cheating in his production methods and of producing candles which did not meet the standard; and that the *muḥtasib* had then sealed his shop. The *ᶜudūl* and *ahl al-khibrah* brought in a sample candle which was examined before the *qāḍī* and in the presence of the *shaykh* and the *muḥtasib*, and found to be free of flaws. The *qāḍī* ordered the *shaykh* and the *muḥtasib* not to interfere further with the plaintiff.[92]

• The *shaykh* and members of the *ṭā'ifah* of the sugar refiners complained that the *muḥtasib* was trying to force them to use as a measure a *raṭl* (pound) of 150 *dirhams*.[93] The plaintiffs presented a *ḥujjah* issued by the previous *qāḍī ᶜaskar* and a *fatwah* signed by the four *muftīs* stating that the *raṭl* of the sugar refiners was 144 *dirhams* and that any inspection of their weighing units must be made by the *qāḍī*, not the *muḥtasib*. The *qāḍī* ordered the *muḥtasib* not to intervene in the affairs of the *ṭā'ifah*.[94]

The amount of tax to be collected from a particular *ṭā'ifah* was also agreed upon in court. For example, the *shaykh* of the *ṭā'ifah* of the coffee-shop owners agreed that the tax on each coffee shop was one *para* per business day.[95] If a *multazim* tried to subject *ṭawā'if* to extra levies, or intervened in their affairs, the case was brought before the *qāḍī*:

• A group from the *ṭā'ifah* of the Nile fishermen complained that the *multazim* had been trying to subject them to a new levy. The *multazim* presented a document stating that the fishermen were supposed to pay three *niṣfs* as a tax plus one *niṣf* for every thirty *niṣfs* of fish sales. The fishermen agreed to that, and the *multazim* agreed not to charge them more.[96]

• The *shaykh* and *usṭahs* from the *ṭā'ifah* of the dyers complained that the *multazim* had forced them to buy the starch he sold to use in their dying operations. The group stated that the starch he produced was inferior and burned the cloth, and that the custom was that each dyer produced his own starch from good rice and wheat. The *qāḍī* warned the *multazim* that if he forced his starch on the dyers, he would be punished.[97]

Finally, disputes regarding distribution of materials or goods and permissions to open new shops by new *usṭahs* were heard by the *qāḍī*, who enforced the *qānūn* of the *ṭā'ifah*.

• The *shaykh* and members of the *ṭā'ifah* of the paper merchants accused two other members of distributing a shipment of pencils among themselves without the knowledge of the *shaykh*. The *shaykh* confirmed the allegations and stated that the defendants had acted against the *qānūn* of the *ṭā'ifah*. The *qāḍī* ordered the defendants to turn over the shipment to the *shaykh* for distribution among all the members.[98]

• A bracelet-maker claimed that the *shaykh* and other members of his *ṭā'ifah* had prevented him from practicing his craft. He stated that he had mastered the craft and had requested that the *shaykh* allow him to be an *usṭah* and open his own shop, but that the *shaykh* had refused him permission. The *shaykh* admitted the charges and claimed that the plaintiff had produced bracelets in his home and had tried to hire away workers of other bracelet-makers, in violation of the *qānūn* of the craft. The two parties agreed, however, that the plaintiff could open his own shop on the condition that he would not produce bracelets in his home, that he would not try to entice workers from other bracelet-makers, and that he would obey the orders of the *shaykh*.[99]

Clearly, the court played an important role in all aspects of urban administration. Disputes related to changes in the structure or function of a building or in the physical makeup of a *ḥārah*, which in pre-Ottoman times were handled by the *muḥtasib*, were now heard by the *qāḍī*. Although the urban population was mainly organized along ethnic, religious, or occupational lines in homogeneous *ḥārahs*, peoples of mixed religious backgrounds frequently lived side by side and interacted socially and economically. The *qāḍī* heard community disputes related to security, standards of morality, and community services; and applied the *Sharīᶜah* to cases in which the religious freedom of non-Muslims was violated by Muslims or other non-Muslims. The *qāḍī* also enforced the social limitations imposed upon non-Muslims.

Merchants and artisans were organized into voluntary *ṭawā'if* and the state through the *qāḍī* not only respected the independence of their members in electing and deposing their *shaykhs*, but also enforced the *qānūns* of the *ṭawā'if* and protected the members against oppression by the *multazims* and *muḥtasibs*.

Chapter IX

RURAL ADMINISTRATION AND THE ADMINISTRATION OF THE AWQĀF

The court also had an active place in rural administration, cultivation, and taxation, and in the establishment and maintenance of private and public *awqāf*.

RURAL ADMINISTRATION

A letter appointing a provincial governor instructed him to maintain order and security, to protect the peasants in their person and property, and to collect the taxes and transmit them to the treasury.[1] The provincial administration policed and defended the countryside against nomadic raids, supervised the cultivation of land, maintained the irrigation canals, and collected taxes--in cash and in kind--and delivered them to the state treasury and the imperial granary.[2] The provincial governors had military regiments stationed in the countryside, and were assisted by *multazims*, village *shaykhs*, *khūlīs* (canal supervisors), and *ghafīrs* (village guards).

The *qāḍī*'s function was to make sure that every official, including the governor, performed his duties according to the *qānūns* of the sultan. A *qāḍī*'s letter of appointment, which instructed him to administer justice, to supervise the maintenance of irrigation canals, and to apply the *Sharīᶜah* and the *qānūns* of the sultan, stated that only he was permitted to hear cases and that those who acted against his decisions would be punished.[3]

When a new governor was appointed, a letter was sent to the *qāḍī* of the province requesting that he supervise the transfer of the office to the new governor or his representative.[4] The *qāḍī* in turn summoned the retiring governor, informed him of the change, and requested that he turn over the gunpowder, arms, ships (used for transporting the taxes paid in kind) and the irrigation canals.[5]

The new governor began his term by appointing *khūlīs* to maintain the irrigation canals. These came to court to affirm their responsibility to preserve the canals from the effects of running water and accruing silt and to dredge them and keep them clean. The *khūlīs* also agreed to receive their salaries from the governor,[6] although some *khūlīs* were exempted from certain taxes as compensation for their services.[7] The *khūlīs* supervised the major canals, which were maintained at state expense and were called *al-jusūr al-sulṭāniyyah* (royal canals).[8] Minor canals were maintained collectively by the villages benefitting from them and were called *al-jusūr al-baladiyyah* (local canals).[9] Because the *al-jusūr al-sulṭāniyyah* were maintained by *waqf* revenues, they were closely supervised by the court. If a community was unable to maintain the *al-jusūr al-baladiyyah*, it petitioned the *wālī* to maintain the canal at state expense. If the community was found after court investigation to be unable to maintain the canal, the *wālī* ordered the provincial governor and the *qāḍī* to maintain the canal at state expense.[10]

The governor also appointed *ghafīrs* to maintain order in the village. Here again, those appointed affirmed their responsibility before the *qāḍī*.[11]

Like the *ḥārah* in the city, the village community was actively involved in maintaining security and basic services:

• A group of cultivators complained to the *qāḍī* that the *nāẓir* of a *waqf* established to maintain the village mosque, a water fountain, and a drinking pool for animals, had diverted the funds to another use. Upon confirmation of the charges by the *ᶜudūl*, the *waqf* was restored to the village and a new *nāẓir* appointed by the *qāḍī*.[12]

• *Multazims* complained that a neighboring *multazim* had blocked the canal which had irrigated their land for a long time, and the land had dried out. The *ᶜudūl* questioned the *shaykhs* of the area and the peasants, and upon confirmation, the defendant was summoned to court, where he was made to declare that he would not block the canal.[13]

The *multazims* had a personal interest in the prosperity of their villages. Under the system of land tenure in seventeenth century Egypt, the *multazims*, in return for a fixed amount to be paid to the state annually, were authorized to collect the taxes imposed on the peasants.[14]

Orders to collect taxes were usually sent jointly to the provincial governor and the *qāḍī*.[15] Once the orders were announced publicly, the *multazims* collected the taxes from the peasants, directly or through *wakīls* or the village *shaykh*.[16] When the taxes were paid, the *multazims* went before the court and released the peasants from their obligations.[17] The *multazims* turned over the taxes to the governor, who in turn delivered the cash to the treasury and the grain to the imperial granary. A record was then issued in court.[18]

Disputes between the governor and the *multazims* over taxes could be brought to the court either directly or through the *wālī*. If a taxpayer refused to pay, the governor could confiscate his property until payment was made. In such cases, the governor asked the *qāḍī* to send the *ᶜudūl* to inventory the items confiscated:

• The governor of al-Bahnasā informed the *qāḍī* that some residents of his province were grazing their sheep in the area, but ran away and hid in a nearby valley each time he tried to collect the taxes. He asked that the *ᶜudūl* be sent with him to count the sheep and cattle and assess the amount of the tax due the state. The *ᶜudūl*, the governor, and a number of *multazims* and military officers made the assessment, and 720 sheep were confiscated.[19]

In other cases, the governor confiscated the animals directly and then reported to the court. After taxes were paid, a settlement was made in court and the governor returned the confiscated animals to their owner.[20]

Multazims who were in debt could request permission from the *wālī* to pay their debts, including state taxes, in annual instalments. The *wālī* then referred the case to the *qāḍī*, who investigated and set up a payment plan.

The *qāḍī* also heard disputes between the *multazims* and the peasants, and between the peasants and the village *shaykh*:

• Two peasants informed the *qāḍī* that the *multazim* was trying to subject them to a levy in addition to the usual land tax and that such a levy had never been paid by them or their ancestors. When two *shuhūd* testified in support of these claims, the *qāḍī* ordered the defendant to collect no more than the customary tax.[21]

• The *shaykh* of a village accused a peasant of refusing to pay *al-ᶜādah* (an annual tax paid in addition to the land tax). The defendant admitted the charges but claimed that he had received the land from his father and that he had been cultivating it for thirty years without paying anything more than the land tax. The peasant produced two *shuhūd* from the village who testified in support of his claims, and the *qāḍī* ordered the *shaykh* not to collect more than the land tax.[22]

ADMINISTRATION OF THE *AWQĀF*

At the time of the Ottoman conquest of Egypt, the number of properties in *waqf* was considerable. The largest were established by the Mamluk sultans for the maintenance of the Muslim Holy Cities of Mecca and Medina; for religious and charitable institutions; and for basic services in urban and rural communities.[23]

After the conquest, the Ottomans made an extensive investigation of all the *awqāf*. Those supported by proper documentation were confirmed, the rest were confiscated, and a register was established for all the *awqāf* in Egypt.[24] Supervision of the *awqāf* was assigned to the *qāḍī ᶜaskar*, who appointed a *nāẓir al-nuẓẓār* (chief supervisor) to monitor the individual *nāẓirs*.[25] A *nāẓir* was appointed directly from Istanbul for the great *awqāf* established by the Mamluk sultans, as well as the ones established later by the Ottoman sultans.[26]

Under the Ottomans, new *awqāf* continued to be established for a variety of purposes. The *awqāf* established by the Ottoman sultans were mainly for the maintenance of the Muslim Holy Cities.[27] *Awqāf* were established, by bureaucrats[28] and others,[29] Muslims and non-Muslims, men and women,[30] partly for the benefit of the founders and their descendants and partly for religious and charitable institutions and for the maintenance of community services such as mosques, schools, public baths, fountains, caravansaries, water wheels, grinding mills, and irrigation canals.

The *waqfiyyah* (charter) of a *waqf* was registered before the *qāḍī*. A typical *waqfiyyah* began by describing the property or properties concerned and the terms by which the *nāẓir* might disburse the revenues. The *waqfiyyah* of a *waqf* established by a military officer for the benefit of a school, a mosque, and a water fountain stated that the *nāẓir* must appoint a man to recite the *Qur›ān* in the mosque twice a day, at a salary of 120 *niṣfs* monthly; another man to call people to prayer and to lead prayer five times a day, at a salary of 90 *niṣfs* per month; a guard to watch over the mosque, clean it, and maintain the water fountain, at a salary of 60 *niṣfs* per month; and in the school, a teacher to teach the students--twenty Muslim orphans--reading, writing, and *Qur'ān* reciting, at a salary of 30 *niṣfs* per month, plus two loaves of bread a day. Each student would receive 10 *niṣfs* per month plus two loaves of bread daily. During the month of Ramaḍān the *nāẓir* was to provide the students with cloth plus the cost of tailoring. He also had to buy oil daily for lighting the mosque. During the month of Ramaḍān oil and candles would be purchased for lighting. The *nāẓir* had to maintain the equipment necessary for the upkeep of the mosque and the school, such as mops, brooms, lamps, rugs, and mats, and see to it that the students were protected against cold and hot weather.[31]

In this case, the principal property was privately owned by the founder. If the property was owned by the state, as was all agricultural land, the land could not be placed in *waqf* without permission from the sultan or the *wālī*.[32] In one such case, the governor of al-Munūfiyyah submitted a petition to the *wālī* stating that he had built a mosque, an inn, a water fountain, a pool for watering animals, and a stable for the benefit of people performing the Pilgrimage. He also had reclaimed fifty acres of waste land near the complex and requested that the revenue from the land be placed in *waqf* to maintain these places and the staff needed for their upkeep. The *wālī* ordered the *qāḍī* of the province to report on the project, and two *ᶜudūl* were dispatched to make a detailed report of the facilities. The *wālī* then granted permission for the establishment of a *waqf*.[33]

Awqāf established in the cities were usually a complex of businesses, the revenue of which was used for public services, such as mosques, baths, and water fountains. The *waqf* of one military officer included houses, a grinding mill, a coffee shop, stores, and a bath.[34] *Awqāf* established by another military officer included nineteen houses and twenty-eight stores; the rental revenue was devoted to maintaining a mosque-school.[35] *Awqāf* established by non-Muslims were usually for maintaining churches and temples, or supporting the non-Muslim poor, or for cleaning the streets of Jerusalem.[36]

The founder of the *waqf* usually appointed himself as *nāẓir* during his lifetime, to be succeeded by his descendants in perpetuity.[37] Upon the death, resignation, or discharge of the *nāẓir*, a new *nāẓir* was appointed by the *qāḍī* according to the terms of the *waqfiyyah*.[38] If the family became extinct, the *qāḍī* could appoint anyone he saw fit and assign the family share of the revenues to a charitable or religious purpose consonant with that of the founder.[39]

The main functions of the *nāẓir* were to rent out the *waqf* properties, collect the revenues, and spend them according to the terms set by the founder. Agricultural land was generally rented for a year,[40] urban properties in three-year increments for up to ninety years. The *nāẓir* was supposed to obtain permission from the *qāḍī* *ᶜaskar* to enter into a long-term contract, in order to discourage deals between *nāẓirs* and tenants for long-term rentals at low rent, and bribes of the *nāẓir*. The rental contracts were so worded as to allow future increases if circumstances changed.[41]

The *nāẓirs* also had to appoint large numbers of *Qur'ān* reciters, teachers, guards, bath attendants, water fountain attendants, scribes, and whatever other employees the founder had authorized.[42] The appointments were confirmed by the *qāḍī*.

Most *waqfiyyahs* stipulated that the *nāẓir* must spend any amounts necessary for the maintenance of the buildings belonging to the *waqf* before distributing the revenue to the beneficiaries.[43] The state also made sure that the *awqāf* were maintained, since most services, both urban and provincial, were supported by *awqāf*. The *wālī* regularly instructed the *qāḍīs* and their *nā'ibs* to inspect the public facilities supported by *awqāf* and to order the *nāẓirs* to make any necessary repairs. *Nāẓirs* who refused to comply were to be reported to the *wālī*.[44] In some cases the *qāḍī* himself went with the building inspectors:

• The *qāḍī* found a crack in the ceiling of a mosque; the building inspector estimated repairs at 50,000 *niṣfs*, and the *qāḍī* ordered the *nāẓir* to proceed with the repairs.[45]

• A *nāẓir* came to court to request permission of the *qāḍī* to proceed with extensive repairs. The *ᶜudūl* and a building inspector examined the *waqf*, the inspector estimated the cost of repairs at 75,000 *niṣfs*, and the *qāḍī* granted permission.[46]

Occasionally, repairs were a subject of dispute between the *nāẓir* and the beneficiaries:

• Two beneficiaries in a family *waqf* accused the *nāẓir* of refusing to pay them their share of the revenue. The *nāẓir* admitted the charges but stated that the *waqf* was in a state of ruin and that after an inspection the previous *qāḍī* had ordered the *nāẓir* to spend whatever was necessary for its restoration. The *nāẓir* said that further repairs still had to be made. Upon presentation of a document to that effect, the *qāḍī* informed the plaintiffs that maintenance of the *waqf*[47] had priority and the case was dropped.

If the revenue was inadequate for repairing the *waqf*, the *nāẓir* occasionally resorted to other means:

- An old mosque had columns covered with marble. When, with the passage of time, the marble overlay fell off, the *nāẓir* petitioned the *qāḍī* for permission to sell the falling marble and use the proceeds to repair the mosque. After architects examined the mosque, the *qāḍī* granted his permission.[48]
- A previous *nāẓir* had staffed the *waqf* with employees in excess of the number authorized by the founder. The new *nāẓir*, with the permission of the *qāḍī*, dismissed the excess workers to provide the *waqf* with cash for its renovation.[49]

The most important check on the *nāẓirs* came from the community which benefitted from the *waqf*. Complaints by the people of a *ḥārah* or a village often resulted in the dismissal of the *nāẓir* and the appointment of another, on condition that he renovate or maintain the facilities.

Finally, each *nāẓir* was supposed to submit to the *qāḍī* an annual statement of *waqf* revenues and disbursements.[50] *Nāẓirs* of *awqāf* established for the Holy Cities in Arabia delivered the net income to the commander of the Pilgrimage.[51]

Thus, in addition to his other duties, the *qāḍī* had to make sure that all rural officials, including the governor, performed their duties according to the *qānūns*. He also heard all disputes regarding security of the village, facilities needed for cultivation, and taxation. The *qāḍī* also protected endowed properties and the rights of individuals and groups connected with *awqāf*. Such functions gave him the right to examine the records of the *awqāf*, to discharge *nāẓirs* who violated the terms of the *awqāf* or neglected the properties, and to authorize repairs.

Chapter X

AN IDEAL DOCTRINE FOR A REAL SOCIETY

The courts of Ottoman Egypt made that "ideal doctrine for an ideal society," the *Sharīᶜah*, a vital part of every citizen's life. The *Sharīᶜah* provided a solid theoretical foundation for the practical application of law to legal problems. And because the *Sharīᶜah* regulated so many areas of men's relations with each other, the courts of Ottoman Egypt were deeply involved in the day-to-day life of everyday Egyptians: deciding whether the placement of a door invaded a neighbor's privacy, whether a convert to Islam had or had not reneged, whether a *multazim* had overstepped the bounds of his authority.

The *Sharīᶜah* was not the only law applied in the courts of Ottoman Egypt, but it was central, and the existence of four different philosophical approaches to the *Sharīᶜah* gave the *qāḍīs* some options in applying the law flexibly to the peculiar needs of particular cases. The *qānūns* of the sultan, which were also applied in the Ottoman Egyptian courts, similarly grew from the *Sharīᶜah* but expanded upon it, as in their extension of the interest ceiling to 10 per cent.

There was surprising equality in the standards of justice of Ottoman Egypt. Men and women, Muslims and non-Muslims could be heard, could serve as witnesses, could be brought to the court to give an account of their actions. Governors and peasants had similar rights, and if the first punished the second without a hearing, the *qāḍī* could hear the peasant's complaint, and act.

Every aspect of life in Ottoman Egypt reveals itself in these seventeenth-century court registers. We learn about the community solidarity of neighborhoods, as neighbors come to seek the eviction of one who threatens their moral standards, or ask the court to force a *nāẓir* to maintain local services provided for by the *waqf* he administered. We learn about the economic life of the time in the enforcement of the sultan's *qānūns* to protect society against fraud in weights, measures, and quality, and to protect the integrity of each trade by holding guild members to the standards imposed by their *ṭawā'if*.

The court registers seem surprisingly contemporary: Divorce, child support, tax problems, environmental problems, privacy, theft, consumer problems--all are brought to the *qāḍī*. Occasionally, then as now, the letter of the law is used to avoid the spirit, as when legal formulas were used in contracts to achieve ends of which the law might disapprove. And occasionally, too, an angry plaintiff brought a frivolous case to court just to harass the defendant.

The seventeenth century registers show us an Ottoman Egypt that differs markedly from that described by so many others in the last fifty years. Given the stereotypes of Islamic despotism, the courts were surprisingly free of executive intervention, remarkably even-handed in the administration of justice. The *qāḍīs* reasoned from the case before them to the *Sharīᶜah* and back again, and in so doing, they proved that this could be an ideal doctrine for a very real society.

APPENDIX

Appendix A

The Courts of Cairo

Court[1]	*Dates*[2]	*Mosque-School*[3]
al-Bāb al-ᶜĀlī	1530-1910	
Būlāq	1536-1811	al-Zīnī
Miṣr al-Qadīmah	1527-1810	al-Nāṣirī
al-Ṣāliḥiyyah	1527-1811	al-Ṣāliḥiyyah
al-Ṣāliḥ	1546-1811	al-Ṣāliḥ
al-Ḥākim	1537-1810	al-Ḥākim
Ṭūlūn	1530-1811	Ibn Ṭūlūn
Qūṣūn	1556-1811	Qūṣūn
al-Zāhid	1546-1811	al-Zāhid
Qanāṭir al-Sibāᶜ	1550-1811	Bard Bek
Bāb al-Shaᶜriyyah	1548-1811	al-Maḥkamah
Bāb al-Saᶜādah wa al-Kharq	1580-1796	Bāb al-Saᶜādah
al-Barmashiyyah	1565-1715	Taghrī Burmush
al-Qismah al-ᶜAskariyyah	1558-1875	al-Ẓāhiriyyah
al-Qismah al-ᶜArabiyyah	1562-1880	al-Kāmiliyyah

THE PROVINCIAL COURTS

Court	*Province*[4]
Alexandria	Alexandria
Rosetta	Rosetta
Damietta	Damietta
Lower Egypt:	
al-Gharbiyyah	al-Maḥallah al-Kubrā, Ziftah, Sindyūn, al-Naḥāriyyah, Sinbwā, Maḥallat Abā ᶜĀlī, Maḥallat Mūrhūm Fuwwah, and al-Burullus
al-Manṣūrah	al-Manṣūrah, al-Wāḥ, al-Munzalah
al-Sharqiyyah	Bilbīs
al-Munūfiyyah	Ibyār, Shalshamūn
al-Qalyūbiyya	al-Khankah
al-Biḥīrah	Damanhūr
Upper Egypt:	
al-Fayūm	al-Fayūm
al-Jīzah	Minf al-ᶜUlyā, Jīzah

Court	*Province*
al-Bahnasā	Banī Suwayf, Tazmant, al-Fashn, and al-Bahnasā
al-Ashmūnīn (Jirjā)	Minyat Ibn Khaṣīm, Deljā-Ashmūnīn
al-Manfalūṭiyyah (Jirjā)	Manfalūṭ
Asyut (Jirjā)	Asyūṭ, Ȧbū Tīj
Jirjā	Jirjā, Qinā-Quṣ, al-Manshiyyah, and Ṭahṭa

Appendix B

The Judicial Hierarchy[1]

The sixth rank (al-Rutbah al-Sādisah)	Cairo, Old Cairo (Miṣr al-Qadīma), Būlāq, Alexandria, Rosetta, Damietta, al-Manṣūrah, al-Maḥallah al-Kubrā, and Minf al-ᶜUlyā
The fifth rank (al-Rutbah al-Khāmisah)	al-Jīzah, Damanhūr, Banī Suwayf, Bilbīs, al-Fayūm, and Ibyār
The fourth rank (al-Rutbah al-Rābiᶜah)	al-Khankah, Minyat ibn Khaṣīm, Manfalūṭ, Jirjā, Ziftah, and al-Manzalah
The third rank (al-Rutbah al-Thālithah)	Asyūt, Tazmant, Shalshamūn, al-Bahnasā, Sindyūn, and al-Naḥāriyyah
The second rank (al-Rutbah al-Thāniyyah)	Sinbwā, Deljā-Ashmūnīn, al-Fashn, Maḥallat Abā ᶜAlī, Maḥallat Marhūm, and Fuwwah
The first rank (primary) (Rutbat Dukhūl Ūlā)	al-Manshiyyah, Qinā-Qūṣ, al-Wāḥ, and al-Burullus

Appendix C

The Registers

The registers of the courts,[1] housed in the *Sharīᶜah* court archives, are organized into four separate series:

Series	*Court*	*Number of Registers*
First	al-Bāb al-ᶜĀlī	1-559
Second	al-Qismah al-ᶜArabiyyah	1-418
Third	al-Qismah al-ᶜAskariyyah	1-157
Fourth	Būlāq	1-83
	Miṣr al-Qadīmah	84-114
	Qanāṭir al-Sibāᶜ	115-159
	Ṭūlūn	160-239
	Qūṣūn	240-306
	al-Ṣālīh	307-370
	Bāb al-Saᶜādah wa al-Kharq	371-438
	al-Ṣālihiyyah	439-537
	al-Ḥākim	538-581
	Bāb al-Shaᶜriyyah	582-655
	al-Zāhid	656-702
	al-Barmashiyyah	703-717

Register 120 (al-Bāb al-ᶜĀlī)

This register is classified as a register from the Cairene court of al-Bāb al-ᶜĀlī. Careful examination of the register, however, reveals that it belongs to the court of Banī Suwayf in the province of al-Bahnasā. All the incoming letters from the viceroy recorded in the register are addressed to the judge of Banī Suwayf and are concerning administrative matters of the province of al-Bahnasā. All the transactions recorded in the register take place in Banī Suwayf or between people living in the province of al-Bahnasā.

Appendix D

Ottoman Chief Judges in Egypt in the Seventeenth Century

Yaḥyā Zakariyyā (second term)	1009 A.H./1600 A.D.
^{c}Abd al-Wahhāb	1010 A.H./1601 A.D.
^{c}Uthmān Muḥammad (third term)	1010 A.H./1602 A.D.
Muḥammad Maḥmūd	1011 A.H./1603 A.D.
Muḥammad Ḥusayn	1012 A.H./1604 A.D.
Muṣṭafā Muḥammad	1013 A.H./1604 A.D.
Muḥammad ^{c}Abd al-Ghanī	1014 A.H./1605 A.D.
Muṣṭafā Bālī	1015 A.H./1606 A.D.
^{c}Abd al-Bāqī Ṭursun	1015 A.H./1606 A.D.
^{c}Abd al-Jabbār	1017 A.H./1608 A.D.
Muḥammad Yaḥyā	1018 A.H./1609 A.D.
Yaḥyā ^{c}Abd al-Ḥakam	1020 A.H./1611 A.D.
^{c}Abd Allah ^{c}Alī	1021 A.H./1612 A.D.
Ṣāliḥ Sa^{c}ad al-Dīn	1023 A.H./1614 A.D.
Nūḥ al-Anṣārī	1025 A.H./1616 A.D.
al-Sayyid Muḥammad	1026 A.H./1617 A.D.
Muḥammad ^{c}Āshiq	1027 A.H./1618 A.D.
Muḥammad ^{c}Azmī	1029 A.H./1620 A.D.
Muḥammad Jūwī	1030 A.H./1621 A.D.
^{c}Abd al-Karīm	1031 A.H./1622 A.D.
^{c}Abd Allah Muḥammad	1031 A.H./1622 A.D.
Raḍwān al-Muḥtashim	1031 A.H./1622 A.D.
Mūsā Zakariyyā	1033 A.H./1624 A.D.
Muḥammad Riyāḍ	1034 A.H./1625 A.D.
Qāsim al-Kurdī	1035 A.H./1626 A.D.
Muḥammad Qarashilbī	1036 A.H./1627 A.D.
Muḥammad al-Nā'ib	1038 A.H./1628 A.D.
^{c}Alī	1038 A.H./1628 A.D.
Aḥmad al-Mu^{c}īd	1040 A.H./1630 A.D.
Muḥammad Aḥmad	1041 A.H./1631 A.D.
^{c}Abd Allah Maḥmud	1042 A.H./1632 A.D.
^{c}Abd al-Raḥmān Bāqī	1044 A.H./1634 A.D.
Aḥmad Tawfīq	1045 A.H./1635 A.D.
^{c}Abd Allah ^{c}Umar	1046 A.H./1636 A.D.
Aḥmad al-Ḥalabī	1047 A.H./1637 A.D.
Sha^{c}bān al-Busnawī	1049 A.H./1639 A.D.
^{c}Ali ^{c}Umar	1051 A.H./1641 A.D.
Shihāb al-Khafājī	1051 A.H./1641 A.D.

Muḥammad Ḍayfī	1053 A.H./1643 A.D.
Mūsā	1054 A.H./1644 A.D.
Muṣṭafā al-Bakrī	1054 A.H./1644 A.D.
As^{c}ad	1055 A.H./1645 A.D.
Muḥammad Ḥasan	1055 A.H./1645 A.D.
Aḥmad Yaḥyā	1056 A.H./1646 A.D.
Zayn al-Dīn	1056 A.H./1646 A.D.
Muḥammad Ṣun^{c}ī	1057 A.H./1647 A.D.
Raḥmat Allah	1058 A.H./1648 A.D.
Muḥammad Amr Allah	1058 A.H./1648 A.D.
Raḥmat Allah	1059 A.H./1649 A.D.
Muḥammad ^{c}Abd al-Ḥalīm	1060 A.H./1650 A.D.
Muḥammad Ḥassan	1061 A.H./1651 A.D.
Rūḥ Allah	1062 A.H./1652 A.D.
Yaḥyā ^{c}Umar	1062 A.H./1652 A.D.
Muḥammad Luṭf Allah	1063 A.H./1653 A.D.
Muḥammad Ṣādiq	1065 A.H./1654 A.D.
Yaḥyā ^{c}Umar	1066 A.H./1655 A.D.
^{c}Ajam Muḥammad	1068 A.H./1657 A.D.
al-Sayyid Aḥmad	1070 A.H./1659 A.D.
Muḥammad Sa^{c}īd	1073 A.H./1662 A.D.
Abū al-Faḍl Aḥmad	1074 A.H./1663 A.D.
Muḥammad Sa^{c}īd	1074 A.H./1663 A.D.
Abū al-Ma^{c}ālī Aḥmad	1075 A.H./1664 A.D.
Abū al-Irshād Sulaymān	1076 A.H./1665 A.D.
Aḥmad Abū al-Ma^{c}ālī	1076 A.H./1665 A.D.
Muṣṭafā ^{c}Abd al-Ḥalīm	1077 A.H./1666 A.D.
Yaḥyā	1079 A.H./1668 A.D.
Muṣṭafā	1080 A.H./1669 A.D.
Muḥammad Nūr Allah	1082 A.H./1671 A.D.
Muḥammad Ṣāliḥ	1083 A.H./1672 A.D.
Burhān al-Dīn	1083 A.H./1672 A.D.
^{c}Abd al-Bāqī Yaḥyā	1084 A.H./1673 A.D.
Muṣṭafā Kabirī	1085 A.H./1674 A.D.
Muḥammad	1086 A.H./1675 A.D.
^{c}Abd al-Bāqī	1087 A.H./1676 A.D.
Hifẓī ^{c}Abd al-Raḥman	1088 A.H./1677 A.D.
Muṣṭafā	1092 A.H./1681 A.D.
^{c}Alī	1095 A.H./1683 A.D.
Ja^{c}far	1098 A.H./1686 A.D.
Muḥammad Ṣādiq	1102 A.H./1690 A.D.
^{c}Ārif ^{c}Abd al-Baqī	1104 A.H./1692 A.D.

NOTES

CHAPTER I: "AN IDEAL DOCTRINE FOR AN IDEAL SOCIETY"

1. Abraham L. Udovitch, *Partnership and Profit in Medieval Islam* (Princeton, 1970), pp. 4-7; and Noel J. Coulson, *History of Islamic Law* (Edinburgh, 1964), pp. 1-7.

2. Joseph Schacht, *The Origins of Muhammadan Jurisprudence* (Oxford, 1950), and "Pre-Islamic Background and Early Development of Jurisprudence," in M. Khadduri and J.H. Liebesny, eds., *Law in the Middle East* (Washington, 1955), pp. 28-56; and Coulson, pp. 75-85.

3. For works on judicial administration in pre-Ottoman times, see Muḥammad b. ᶜArnūs, *Tārīkh al-Qaḍā' fī al-Islām* (Cairo, 1934); Muḥammad Sallām Madkūr, *al-Qaḍā' fī al-Islām* (Cairo, 1944); Emile Tyan, *Histoire de l'organisation judiciaire en pays d'Islam,* 2 vols. (Leiden, 1959), and "Judicial Organization," in M. Khadduri and J.H. Liebesny, eds., *Law in the Middle East,* pp. 236-78. For the Ottoman period in Egypt, see ᶜAbd al-Raḥīm ᶜAbd al-Raḥīm, "al-Qaḍā' fī Miṣr al-ᶜUthmāniyyah," in the JTM publication, *Buḥūth fī al-Tārīkh al-Ḥadīth* (Cairo, 1976), pp. 171-87. For judicial administration elsewhere in the Ottoman Empire, see R. Jennings, Jr., *The Judicial Registers (Serᶜi Mahkeme Sicilleri) of Kayseri* (Ann Arbor, 1972); and Uriel Heyd, *Studies in Old Ottoman Criminal Law,* ed. V.L. Menage (Oxford, 1973).

4. For a survey of the literary sources for the period, see P.M. Holt, "Ottoman Egypt (1517-1798): An Account of Arabic Historical Sources," in P.M. Holt, ed., *Political and Social Change in Modern Egypt* (London, 1968), pp. 3-12; and Stanford Shaw, "Turkish Source-Materials for Egyptian History," in Holt, ed., *Change in Egypt,* pp. 28-51.

5. For a survey of the political history of Ottoman Egypt, see ᶜAbd al-Karīm Rāfiq, *Bilād al-Shām wa Miṣr (1516-1798)* (Damascus, 1968); and P.M. Holt, "The Pattern of Egyptian Political History from 1517-1798," in Holt, ed., *Change in Egypt*, pp. 79-90.

6. For the different views summarized above, see ᶜAbd al-Raḥīm ᶜAbd al-Raḥīm, *al-Rīf al-Miṣrī fī al-Qarn al-Thāmin ᶜAshar* (Cairo, 1974), pp. 250-63; ᶜAbd al-Raḥman al-Rāfᶜi, *Tārīkh al-Ḥarakah al-Qawmiyyah* (Cairo, 1929), 1:42-43; H.A.R. Gibb and Harold Bowen,

Islamic Society and the West: A Study of the Impact of Western Civilization on Moslem Culture in the Near East (London, 1950), 1:208-9 (unless otherwise indicated, references to Gibb and Bowen are to Part 1); Muḥammad al-Raqīd, *al-Ghazw al-ᶜUthmānī li Miṣr* (Cairo, 1968), pp. 264-66, 300-302; Stanford Shaw, *The Financial and Administrative Organization and Development of Ottoman Egypt (1517-1798)* (Princeton, 1962), pp. 1-3, and *Ottoman Egypt in the Age of the French Revolution* (Cambridge, 1964), p. 3; Bernard Lewis, "The Islamic Guilds," *Economic History Review*, 8(1937-38): 20-37; Gabriel Baer, *Studies in the Social History of Modern Egypt* (Chicago, 1969), pp. 93-94, and sources cited therein; and E. Strauss, "The Social Isolation of Ahl al-Dhimma," *Etudes Orientales*, 1(1950):73-94.

7. Ira M. Lapidus, *Muslim Cities in the Later Middle Ages* (Cambridge, 1967), pp. 96-97.

8. *Ibid.*, pp. 107-15.

9. Gabriel Baer, *Egyptian Guilds in Modern Times* (Jerusalem, 1964), p. 69.

10. *Ibid.*

11. *Ibid.*

12. *Ibid.*, pp. 11-12.

13. See Inalcik's review of the works of Lapidus and Baer in *Archivum Ottomanicum*, 1(1969):317-19. Raymond, who studied the structure of the *ṭawā'if* in eighteenth-century Egypt, maintained that the office of the *shaykh* was elective, but that the government had the right to intervene. This, he claimed, depended on the importance of the *ṭā'ifah* and its ability to resist government intervention. André Raymond, *Artisans et commerçants au Caire au XVIIIe siècle* (Damascus, 1974), 2:550-53.

14. Gibb and Bowen, pp. 208-9.

15. Bigg and Bowen, 2:128; and Heyd, *Ottoman Criminal Law*, pp. 219-21 and "Ḳānūn and Sharīᶜah in Old Ottoman Criminal Justice," *PIASH*, 3(1967):1-18.

16. A.K.S. Lambton has discussed the classical theory of government as discussed by the jurists, administrative and political writers, and philosophers in "Justice in the Medieval Persian Theory of Kingship," *SI*, 17 (1962):91-120. For the Ottoman theory of government, see Halil Inalcik, *The Ottoman Empire: The Classical Age 1300-1600* (London, 1973), pp. 65-69, "The Ottoman Economic Mind," in M.A. Cook, ed., *Studies in the Economic History of the Middle East* (London, 1970), pp. 207-18, "The Nature of Traditional Society--Turkey," in R.E. Ward and Dankwart A. Rustow, eds., *Political Modernization in Japan and Turkey* (Princeton, 1964), pp. 42-62, and "Capital Formation in the Ottoman Empire," *Journal of Economic History*, 29 (1969):97-140; Hubert Darke, tr., *The Book of Government or Rules for Kings: The Siyar al-Muluk or Siyasatnama of Nizam al-Mulk* (London, 1960); and Ihsan Abbas, *ᶜAhd Ardshir* (Beirut, 1967).

17. Lambton, pp. 91-120; and Inalcik, *The Ottoman Empire*, pp. 65-69.

18. Joseph Schacht, *An Introduction to Islamic Law* (Oxford, 1964), pp. 49-56; Coulson, pp. 120-34; and Tyan, "Judicial Organization," pp. 236-78.

19. Coulson, pp. 123-34.
20. *Ibid.*
21. Halil Inalcik, "Örf," *IA*; Uriel Heyd, *Ottoman Criminal Law*, pp. 168-71; and Farhat J. Ziadeh, "Urf and Law in Islam," *The World of Islam: Studies in Honour of P.K. Hitti* (London, 1959), pp. 60-67.
22. *EI*^{2} s.v. "Ḳānūn" and "Ḳānūnnāme" by H. Inalcik; and "Istiḥsān," by R. Paret; and Schacht, *Muhammadan Jurisprudence*, pp. 99-115.
23. Inalcik, "Ḳānūn" and "Ḳānūnnāme."
24. *Ibid.*
25. Ibn Taymiyyah, *al-Siyāsah al-Shar*^{c}*iyyah fī Iṣlāḥ al-Ra*^{c}*ī wa al-Ra*^{c}*iyyah* (Cairo, 1951); Coulson, p. 129; and Heyd, *Ottoman Criminal Law*, pp. 198-207.
26. Inalcik, "Ḳānūn" and "Ḳānūnnāme."
27. Tyan, "Judician Organization," pp. 259-60.
28. *Ibid.*, pp. 269-77.
29. *Ibid.*, pp. 271-73; and *EI*^{2}, "Ḥājib," by E. Tyan.
30. The *shurṭah* was charged with maintaining public order and executing penalties. The head of the *shurṭah* was also authorized to investigate crimes, conduct trials, and deliver sentences. Tyan, "Judicial Organization," pp. 274-76.
31. The *muḥtasib*'s main function was to enforce prices, weights, and measures, but he could also punish offenses against religion and morality, such as non-attendance at public prayers and non-fasting. *EI*^{2}, "Hisba," by Claude Cahen and M. Talbi.
32. Madkūr, pp. 141-47.
33. Coulson, p. 130; and *EI*^{2}, s.v. "Ḳānūn" by Y. Linant de Bellefonds; and Tyan, "Judicial Organization," pp. 267-77.
34. Externally, the Mamluk state had been facing military threats from the Crusaders, Ottomans, and Turkmans in the north, the Mongols and Timurids in the east, and the Portuguese in the south. Internally, the central authority was weakened by the rivalry between various factions in the military and the rise of a semi-feudal class of landlords. For a survey of Egypt's political history and foreign relations under the Mamluks, see Ahmad Darrag, *L'Egypt sous le règne de Barsbay, 1422-1438* (Damascus, 1961); Fāyid ^{c}Āshūr, *al-*^{c}*Ilāqāt al-Siyāsiyyah bayn al-Mamālīk wa al-Maghūl fī al-Dawlah al-Mamlūkiyyah al-Ūlā* (Cairo, 1974); Muḥammad Surūr, *Dawlat Banī¯qalāwūn fī Miṣr* (Cairo, 1947); Sa^{c}īd ^{c}Āshūr, *al-*^{c}*Aṣr al-Mamālīkī fī Miṣr wa al-Shām* (Cairo, 1962); and John Woods, *The Aqquyunlu: Clan, Confederation, Empire* (Minneapolis and Chicago, 1976).
35. For the conditions of subjects in Mamluk Egypt, see Sa^{c}id ^{c}Āshūr, *al-Mujtama*^{c} *al-Miṣrī fī* ^{c}*Aṣr Salāṭīn al-Mamālīk* (Cairo, 1962) and "al-Fallāḥ wa al-Iqṭā^{c} fī ^{c}Aṣr al-Ayyūbīyin wa al-Mamālīk," in JTM publication, *al-Arḍ wa al-Fallāh fī Miṣr* ^{c}*alā marr al-*^{c}*uṣūr* (Cairo, 1974), pp. 210-24; David Ayalon, "The Great Yāsa of Chingiz Khan: A Re-Examination," *SI* 38(1973):110-27; and Nazīr Sa^{c}dāwī, *Ṣuwar wa Maẓālim min* ^{c}*Aṣr al-Mamālīk* (Cairo, 1966), pp. 31-53.
36. For the Ottoman organization of Egypt see Ö.L. Barkan, *XV ve XVI-inci asirlarda Osmanli Impratorlugunda Zirai Ekonomimin*

Hukuki ve Mali Esaslari-Kanunlar (Istanbul, 1945), pp. 335-95; Halil Inalcik, "Adaletnameler," *Belgeler*, 2(1967):44-63, and "Ottoman Methods of Conquest," *SI* 2(1954):103-29; ᶜAbd al-Raḥīm, *al-Rīf al-Miṣrī*, pp. 1-63; Shaw, *Financial Administration*, pp. 12-58, and "The Land Law of Ottoman Egypt (960-1553); A Contribution to the Study of Landholding in the Early Years of Ottoman Rule in Egypt," *Der Islam*, 38(1962):106-37; and Heyd, *Ottoman Criminal Law*, pp. 1-33.

CHAPTER II: THE COURT REGISTERS

1. For surveys and studies of the registers of the *Sharīᶜah* courts, see Appendix C; ᶜAbd al-Raḥīm ᶜAbd al-Raḥīm, *al-Rīf al-Miṣrī*, pp. 39, 301; André Raymond, "Les documents du Mahkama comme source pour l'histoire economique et sociale de l'Egypte au XVIIIe siècle," in Jacques Berque et Dominique Chevalier, *Les Arabes par leurs Archives: XVIe-XXe Siècles* (Paris, 1976), pp. 125-40; Daniel Crecelius, "The Organization of *Waqf* Documents in Cairo," *IJMES*, 2(1970):266-77; Salwā Mīlād, "Sijillāt Maḥkamat al-Bāb al-ᶜĀlī: Dirāsah Arshīfiyyah Diplūmātiyyah" (Ph.D. dissertation, Cairo University, 1975); and Stanford Shaw, "Cairo's Archives and the History of Ottoman Egypt," *Report on Research, Spring, 1956* (Washington, 1956), pp. 59-72.
2. Crecelius, p. 18; and Mīlād, pp. 245-46.
3. BR, Reg. 711, p. 1.
4. SH, Reg. 519, p. 2.
5. BA, Reg. 125, Docs. 513-20.

CHAPTER III: THE COMPOSITION OF THE JUDICIARY

1. The number of provinces in Ottoman Egypt (923 A.H./1517-1300 A.H./1882) changed from time to time. In the seventeenth century, the provinces were Cairo, Alexandria, Rosetta, Ḍamietta, al-Gharbiyyah, al-Sharqiyyah, al-Munūfiyyah, al-Biḥīrah, al-Manṣūrah, al-Qalyubiyyah, Fāraskūr, Ṭarrānah, al-Waḥḥāt, al-Manzalah, al-Jīzah, al-Fayyum, ᶜAtfīh, al-Bahnasā, al-Ashmūniyyah, al-Manfalūtiyyah, al-Minyah, Asyūṭ, Jirjā, and Aswān. Shaw, *Financial Administration*, pp. 14-16; ᶜAbd al-Raḥīm, *al-Rīf al-Miṣrī*, pp. 7-18; and Muḥammad Ramzī, *al-Qāmūs al-Jughrāfī* (Cairo, 1954-63), 5 vols.
2. See Appendix A.
3. *Ibid.*
4. The exact number of courts in Cairo during the Ottoman period is not known. Registers exist for fifteen courts (see Appendix C). These registers indicate three additional Cairene courts (al-Azbakiyyah, al-Ḍawāḥī, and Jazīrat al-Fīl) from which no records were found. BA, Reg. 126, Doc. 910; ᶜAbd al-Raḥīm, *al-Rīf al-Miṣrī*, p. 39; and Mīlād, p. 125.
5. Stanford Shaw puts the total number of districts and courts in Egypt during the Ottoman period at eighty, but does not cite his sources; Shaw, *Financial Administration*, p. 59.

Aḥmad al-^{c}Arīshī, Egyptian *qāḍī ^{c}askar* during the French occupation of Egypt (1213 A.H./1798 A.D.-1218 A.H./1803 A.D.), reporting to the French authorities on judicial administration, gave only the names of the main courts, and stated that each *qāḍī* appointed as many *nā'ibs* as were necessary in his district. C.A. Bachatly, "L'administration de la justice en Egypt à la veille des réformes de l'an IX, d'après un document arabe inédit," *BIE* 18(1935):1-18.

6. Bachatly, pp. 1-18; and Appendix B. For the larger Ottoman judicial hierarchy, see Gibb and Bowen, 2:121-32; and Inalcik, *The Ottoman Empire*, pp. 170-72.

7. ^{c}Alī Mubārak, *al-Khiṭaṭ al-Tawfīqiyyah* (Cairo, 1888), 16:88-89; and Shaw, *Ottoman Egypt*, pp. 95-97.

8. SH, Reg. 519, p. 1; BU, Reg. 59, p. 2.

9. Before leaving Cairo in 923 A.H./1517 A.D., Sultan Salīm appointed a trustee with the title of *al-Qassām al-^{c}Arabī* to administer the inheritances of non-members of the bureaucracy, and in 929 A.H./1522 A.D. *al-Qassām al-^{c}Askarī* (the military trustee) was sent to Cairo to administer the inheritance of the members of the bureaucracy. He also presided over al-Ṣāliḥiyyah. But in 966 A.H./1558 A.D. and 970 A.H./1562 A.D., the two courts of al-Qismah al-^{c}Askariyyah and al-Qismah al-^{c}Arabiyyah were established. See Ibn Iyās, *Bada'i^{c} al-Zuhūr fī waqā'i^{c} al-Duhūr* (Cairo, 1961), pp. 165, 451-59; QS, Reg. 1, p. 1; QA, Reg. 1, p. 1.

10. BF, Reg. 120, Doc. 212.

11. Mīlād, pp. 129-30.

12. Muslim jurists were split on the issue of placing courts inside the mosques. The Shāfi^{c}ī school opposed the idea because it might disturb the prayer, but the Ḥanafī and Mālikī schools sanctioned the practice because administering justice was an act of faith. Emile Tyan, "Judicial Organization," p. 244; ^{c}Arnūs, p. 125. The practice of placing courts in mosques was begun in Egypt in 1015 by the *qāḍī* Abū al-^{c}Abbās al-Sa^{c}dī. Ibn Ḥajar al-^{c}Asqalānī, *Raf^{c} al-Iṣr ^{c}An Quḍāt Miṣr* (Cairo, 1957), p. 105.

13. Mīlād, pp. 137-41. In the court of al-Bāb al-^{c}Ālī, located in a palace, the *qāḍī ^{c}askar* and the *nā'ibs* sat in one hall.

14. Mīlād, pp. 137-41.

15. Both titles, *qāḍī al-quḍāh* and *qāḍī ^{c}askar*, predated the Ottoman era in Egypt. In Mamluk Egypt (657 A.H./1258 A.D.-923 A.H./1517 A.D.), the two titles designated two different judicial offices with different jurisdictions. The four *qāḍī al-quḍāh*, representing the four schools of jurisprudence, were the chief judges, but their jurisdiction extended only over the civilian population. The Shāf^{c}ī judge was more important than the other three. The four *qāḍī ^{c}askars* presided over cases involving military individuals, and military disputing with civilians. With the Ottoman conquest in 1517, the two offices were combined in the office of the Ottoman *qāḍī ^{c}askar* with jurisdiction over both military and civilians. See Aḥmad al-Qalqashandī, *Ṣubḥ al-A^{c}shā fī Ṣinā^{c}at al-Inshā*, Vol. 4 (Cairo, n.d.), p. 192; and *EI^{2}*, s.v. "Ḳaḍi ^{c}Askar," by E. Tyan and Gy Kaldy Nagy.

16. The *qāḍī ^{c}askar* of Egypt was ranked with the great Mullās (judges of the main cities) on the Ottoman *^{c}ilmiyyah* (religious) hierarchy of grades and posts. At the top of it stood the chief

muftī. Below him came the two *qāḍī ᶜaskars* of Rumelia and Anatolia, then the *qāḍīs* of Istanbul, Mecca, Edirne, Bursa, and Cairo, in graded posts with each post theoretically a prerequisite for the next. Next came the *qāḍīs* of the smaller cities, and finally the *qāḍīs* of the towns. The *qāḍī* of Egypt was thus several ranks below that of a *qāḍī ᶜaskar*. Inalcik, *The Ottoman Empire*, pp. 170-72; Gibb and Bowen, 2:121-23; and Madeline Zilfi, "The Ottoman Ulema 1703-1829 and the Route to Great Mullaship" (Ph.D. dissertation, University of Chicago, 1976), pp. 135-38.

17. The first Egyptian to be *qāḍī ᶜaskar* in Egypt was Aḥmad al-ᶜArīshī, who was appointed by the French in 1799. ᶜAbd al-Raḥman al-Jabartī, *ᶜAjā'ib al-Athar fī al-Tarājim wa al-Akhbār*, 12 vols. (Cairo, 1958), 3:53; Shaw, *Ottoman Egypt*, pp. 95-96; and Bachatly, pp. 1-18. However, one Egyptian-born religious scholar was appointed to the post of *muftī* in Istanbul. Other Egyptians were appointed *qāḍī ᶜaskars* in Damascus. Muḥammad al-Muḥibbī, *Khulaṣāt al-athār fī aᶜyan al-qarn al-ḥādī ᶜashar*, 5 vols. (Beirut, 1966), 1:120-22.

18. Appendix D.

19. During the earlier centuries of Ottoman history, the *qāḍīs* of the main cities were appointed on the recommendation of the *qāḍī ᶜaskar* of Anatolia, but before the end of the sixteenth century, this role was assumed by the grand *muftī*. Michael M. Pixley, "The Development and Role of the Şeyhülislam in Early Ottoman History," *JAOS*, 96(1976):89-96; Zilfi, pp. 4-44.

20. Zilfi, p. 135.

21. To meet the rising demand for high posts, several lower posts (such as Aleppo, Damascus, and Medina) were upgraded. BA, Reg. 123, Doc. 1648; Zilfi, pp. 135-36.

22. Zilfi, pp. 135-36.

23. For example, ᶜAbd Allah b. ᶜUmar, *qāḍī ᶜaskar* of Egypt in 1046 A.H./1636 A.D.-1047 A.H./1637 A.D., in a short time reached the position of teacher at one of the highest schools of the empire and then received Edirne as his first judgeship--according to al-Muḥibbī because his father was the tutor of Sultan ᶜUthmān II. The grand *muftī* at the time, in a meeting with ᶜAbd Allah, made a cynical remark regarding ᶜAbd Allah's fast promotion, to which ᶜAbd Allah replied, "I was not the first case in Islam." Al-Muḥibbī, 3:64. For other cases of Egyptian *qāḍī ᶜaskars* who came from prominent ulema families, see al-Muḥibbī, 1:127-29, 396-98; 3:418-20.

24. According to Stanford Shaw, the *qāḍī ᶜaskar* of Egypt paid 1,235,000 *niṣf* (silver *para*) a year to the *qāḍī ᶜaskar* of Rumelia in return for his position. Shaw, *Ottoman Egypt*, p. 97 (source uncited); Zilfi, pp. 42-44.

25. When ᶜAbd Allah b. Muḥammad, *qāḍī ᶜaskar* of Egypt, died in 1042 A.H./1623 A.D., the *wālī* Khalīl Pashā appointed Mūsā Efendī as substitute until the new *qāḍī* arrived. Muḥammad b. Abī al-Surur al-Bakrī, *al-Kawākib al-Sa'irah fī Akhbār Miṣr wa al-Qāhirah*, British Library MS. Add. 7324, fol. 64-69.

26. When ᶜAbd al-Bāqī Ṭursūn died in Egypt in 1016 A.H./1607 A.D., the *wālī* Hasan Pāshā appointed ᶜAbd al-Jabbār his substitute; ᶜAbd al-Jabbār then served as *qāḍī ᶜaskar* from 1016 A.H./

1607 A.D. to 1017 A.H./1608 A.D. Amīn Sāmī, *Taqwīm al-Nīl* (Cairo, 1928), 2:36.

27. Appendix D.

28. Shaw, *Financial Administration*, p. 2; *Ottoman Egypt*, p. 4.

29. At the beginning of the Ottoman era, the *qāḍī* ᶜ*askar* presided over al-Ṣāliḥiyyah, the seat of the Mamluk chief *qāḍīs*. But in 1530, the court of al-Bāb al-ᶜĀlī was established as a new seat for the head of judicial administration, and al-Ṣāliḥiyyah then became a sub-district court. Ibn Iyās, 5:458-59, and 173.

30. Shaw, *Ottoman Egypt*, p. 96. Some of the provincial *qāḍīs*, however, were Egyptians. Al-Muḥibbī, 3:366; Shaw, *Ottoman Egypt*, p. 96; and ᶜAbd al-Raḥīm, *al-Rīf al-Miṣrī*, pp. 40-42, and "al-Qaḍā' fī Miṣr," p. 180.

31. Al-Muḥibbī, 1:66, 2:175-76, 225, 3:23.

32. ᶜAbd al-Ḥayy al-Kurdī was working for the *wālī* ᶜUwayas Pashā, who appointed him *qāḍī* of al-Jīzah. Al-Muḥibbī, 2:344.

33. QR, Reg. 133, p. 1, Reg. 134, p. 1, Reg. 135, p. 1, Reg. 136, p. 1, Reg. 137; QA, Reg. 144, p. 1; EI^2, s.v. "Kassām," by Cengiz Orhanlu; and O.L. Barkan, "Edirne Askeri Kassamina ait Tereke Defterler, 1545-1659," *Belgeler*, 3(1966):1-479.

34. Al-Muḥibbī, 1:366, 2:175-76.

35. QR, Reg. 134, p. 1, Reg. 135, p. 1, Reg. 137, p. 1, Reg. 138, p. 1, and Reg. 144, p. 1.

36. QR, Reg. 135, p. 1, Reg. 136, p. 6, Reg. 137, p. 1, Reg. 138, p. 1; SH, Reg. 519, p. 2.

37. BA, Reg. 128, p. 1; SA, Reg. 361, p. 2; SH, Reg. 519, p. 1; BU, Reg. 60, p. 1; and BQ, Reg. 424, p. 2.

38. ᶜAbd al-Raḥīm, *al-Qaḍā' fī Miṣr*, p. 178; Shaw, *Ottoman Egypt*, p. 97.

39. BA, Reg. 128, p. 1.

40. Al-Muḥibbī, 4:467-72.

41. *Ibid.*

42. BA, Reg. 128-Reg. 153, p. 1.

43. BA, Reg. 131, p. 5, Reg. 132, p. 6.

44. BA, Reg. 153, p. 1.

45. The Shāfiᶜī *nā'ib* at al-Bāb al-ᶜĀlī was called Muḥammad al-ᶜĀmīlī, BA, Reg. 153, p. 1. Later he was replaced by another Shāfiᶜī *nā'ib* whose name was Shams al-Dīn al-ᶜĀmīlī, BA, Reg. 163, p. 9. Several Egyptian *nā'ibs* were also sons and grandsons of *nā'ibs*, BF, Reg. 120, Docs. 12, 20, 48, 56, 122, 256, 285, and 326.

46. Gibb and Bowen, 2:129; Heyd, *Ottoman Criminal Law*, p. 220; and Inalcik, *The Ottoman Empire*, p. 75.

47. ᶜAbd al-Raḥīm, "Al-Qaḍa' fī Miṣr, pp. 181- 82; *al-Rīf al-Miṣrī*, pp. 24-25; and Inalcik, "Adâletnâmeler," pp. 61-62.

48. Heyd, *Ottoman Criminal Law*, p. 220.

49. Ibrāhīm al-Muwaylḥī, "Al-ᶜArḍ wa al-Fallāḥ fī al-ᶜAṣr al-ᶜUthmānī," in *Al-Arḍ wa al-Fallāḥ fī Miṣr*, JTM (Cairo, 1974), pp. 224-58; Shaw, *Ottoman Egypt*, p. 4, and *Financial Administration*, p. 2.

50. Shaw, *Financial Administration*, p. 2.

51. Heyd, *Ottoman Criminal Law*, p. 220; BA, Reg. 123, Doc. 1648.

52. ᶜAbd al-Raḥīm, "Al-Qaḍā' fī Miṣr," pp. 181-82.

53. *Ibid.*
54. *Ibid.*, pp. 24-25; and Inalcik, "Adâletnâmeler," p. 62.
55. *Ibid.*
56. BR, Reg. 710, p. 2.
57. BR, Reg. 710, p. 2; BU, Reg. 36, p. 1; TU, Reg. 186, pp. 1-3; and TU, Reg. 194, pp. 1-2.
58. BA, Reg. 123, Docs. 1187, 1188, 1477, and 1478.
59. BA, Reg. 121, Doc. 21; Reg. 122, Docs. 583, 1257.
60. BU, Reg. 36, p. 1; TU, Reg. 196, p. 3, and Reg. 194, p. 2.
61. BR, Reg. 710, p. 1; BS, Reg. 629, Doc. 10, Reg. 634, Doc. 1; SA, Reg. 340, p. 1; BR, Reg. 710, p. 2; BS, Reg. 634, Doc. 1; SA, Reg. 361, p. 2; and BU, Reg. 36, p. 1, Reg. 59, p. 2.
62. TU, Reg. 196, p. 1.
63. BU, Reg. 59, p. 1; TU, Reg. 194, p. 3, Reg. 196, p. 3.
64. BA, Reg. 143, last page.
65. BR, Reg. 711, p. 2.
66. BR, Reg. 710, p. 1.

CHAPTER IV: ASPECTS OF COURT ADMINISTRATION

1. BF, Reg. 120, Doc. 338; BA, Reg. 121, Doc. 116, Reg. 122, Doc. 114, Reg. 123, Docs. 1478, 1557, and 1600, Reg. 124, Doc. 14, Reg. 129, Doc. 1191.
2. For the history of the institution of *shahādah*, see Tyan, "Judicial Organization," pp. 253-55.
3. *Ibid.*
4. BU, Reg. 60, p. 1; BS, Reg. 629, Doc. 1.
5. BS, Reg. 629, Doc. 2, Reg. 634, Doc. 11.
6. BS, Reg. 134, Doc. 10; SA, Reg. 361, p. 2.
7. BA, Reg. 143, last page.
8. BA, Reg. 123, Docs. 1187, 1203, and 1205.
9. BA, Reg. 27, Docs. 1002, 1003, 1083, 1084, and 1090; BF, Reg. 120, Docs. 124, 126, 133, 140, and 142.
10. Chapter VI.
11. BA, Reg. 122, Docs. 1330 and 1646, Reg. 123, Doc. 972, Reg. 128, Doc. 1530.
12. BA, Reg. 123, Docs. 1478, 1557, and 1660.
13. BA, Reg. 123, p. 88, Reg. 126, Doc. 249.
14. BA, Reg. 123, Docs. 642, 886, 1085, and 1516.
15. BA, Reg. 119, Doc. 451, Reg. 123, Doc. 1507.
16. BF, Reg. 120, Doc. 207; BA, Reg. 119, Doc. 515, Reg. 125, Doc. 148.
17. BA, Reg. 123, Docs. 893 and 1107; BA, Reg. 125, Doc. 70.
18. BA, Reg. 119, Doc. 451; BA, Reg. 125, Doc. 215.
19. BA, Reg. 119, Doc. 515; BA, Reg. 125, Doc. 148.
20. BA, Reg. 123, Docs. 893 and 1107, Reg. 125, Doc. 70.
21. BA, Reg. 123, Docs. 1161, 1444, and 1778.
22. *Ibid.*
23. BA, Reg. 123, Doc. 1444.
24. BA, Reg. 123, Doc. 1444, Reg. 128, Doc. 1696.
25. BA, Reg. 211, Doc. 190.
26. BA, Reg. 126, Doc. dated 16th Rabī^{c} II, 1648.

27. BA, Reg. 123, Docs. 1636 and 1778.
28. BF, Reg. 120, Docs. 255 and 338.
29. Claude Cahen suggests that lists of individuals qualified as ᶜ*udūl* were compiled in each court, but such lists were not encountered anywhere in the registers. Claude Cahen, "A propos de shuhūd," *SI*, 31(1970):71-79; and Jennings, pp. 54-55. The only list of names found was that of the official ᶜ*udūl* of the court, BA, Reg. 143, last page.
30. BA, Reg. 123, Docs. 1087 and 1088, Reg. 125, Doc. 239, Reg. 126, Doc. 908; BF, Reg. 120, Docs. 207 and 341.
31. BU, Reg. 36, p. 1; TU, Reg. 194, p. 2, Reg. 196, p. 3; BR, Reg. 710, p. 1; BS, Reg. 629, Docs. 1-10; SA, Reg. 361, p. 2.
32. BA, Reg. 123, Docs. 1087 and 1808, Reg. 125, Doc. 239, Reg. 126, Doc. 908.
33. *Ibid.*
34. Jennings has suggested that the *muslimūn* may have been advisors who gave advice (*mashūrah*) to the *qāḍīs*. Jennings, *The Judicial Registers.*
35. BA, Reg. 123, Doc. 1843.
36. BA, Reg. 124, Docs. 325 and 784.
37. BA, Reg. 125, Docs. 283 and 1123.
38. BA, Reg. 124, Docs. 325 and 784, Reg. 125, Docs. 283 and 1123.
39. BA, Reg. 131, pp. 2-3, Reg. 132, p. 1, Reg. 136, Docs. 12 and 13, Reg. 153, p. 4.
40. *Ibid.*
41. BR, Reg. 710, p. 2; BF, Reg. 120, Doc. 2.
42. BR, Reg. 710, p. 2.
43. TU, Reg. 194, p. 2; KU, Reg. 259, Doc. 6; BR, Reg. 710, p. 2.
44. BF, Reg. 120, Docs. 2, 24, 94, and 187.
45. BF, Reg. 120, Doc. 361; BA, Reg. 126, Doc. dated March, 1648.
46. The city of Cairo was made up of walled neighborhoods, each with a gate. A guard appointed by the government stood before each gate. Each village was also assigned a number of guards; see Chapters VIII and IX.
47. Heyd, *Ottoman Criminal Law*, pp. 111-19.
48. BA, Reg. 114, Doc. 175, Reg. 119, Docs. 557 and 1505, Reg. 123, Docs. 1223 and 1417.
49. BA, Reg. 123, Doc. 1443.
50. BA, Reg. 125, Doc. 283.
51. BA, Reg. 121, Doc. 206.
52. BA, Reg. 125, Doc. 701.
53. The police in Egypt were under the direct authority of the chief of the janissary corps. The latter appointed three police officials (*ṣūbāshī* or *wālī*) who were in charge of policing the city with the assistance of a number of soldiers. Police posts were located in various parts of the cities. Each neighborhood was also assigned a night guard. In the villages, police were under the direction of the village head (*shaykh al-balad*), who appointed guards to police the village. André Raymond, "Al-Qāhirah al-ᶜUthmāniyyah be waṣfihā madīnah," tr. Zuhayr al-Shāyib,

MTM, 20(1973):226-29; and Shaw, *Financial Administration*, pp. 148 and 189-90.

54. BA, Reg. 119, Docs. 546, 846, and 1504, Reg. 125, Doc. 69, Reg. 127, Doc. 1747, Reg. 128, Doc. 1696.

55. *Ibid.*

56. *Ibid.*

57. BA, Reg. 127, Doc. 1747.

58. *Ibid.*; and BA, Reg. 128, Doc. 1696.

59. BA, Reg. 119, Doc. 546, Reg. 124, Doc. 325.

60. BA, Reg. 127, Doc. 1747. For the value of the *niṣf*, see Shaw, *Financial Administration*, p. xxii.

61. BA, Reg. 128, Doc. 1696.

62. *Ibid.*

63. BA, Reg. 125, Doc. 214.

64. For the background of the office of the *muftī* and the nature of Ottoman legal *fatwahs*, see Gibb and Bowen, 2:133-38; Uriel Heyd, "Some Aspects of Ottoman Fetwa," *BSOAS*, 32(1969):35-56; and Madkūr, pp. 135-39.

65. ᶜAbd al-Raḥīm, *al-Rīf al-Miṣrī*, p. 44.

66. BU, Reg. 36, p. 1. For fees collected in other parts of the Empire see Halil Inalcik, "Bursa Serᶜiye Sicillerinde Fatih Sultan Mehmed'in Fermanlari," *Beleten*, 11(1947):693-703.

67. BU, Reg. 36, p. 1.

68. TU, Reg. 194, p. 1. Some of these orders suggest that violations did take place.

69. Shaw, *Ottoman Egypt*, p. 97.

70. *Ibid.*

71. The *ardabb* of wheat equalled 14-1/6 bushels. Shaw, *Financial Administration*, p. 79, note; W. Hinz, *Islamische Masse und Gewichte* (Leiden, 1955), p. 39.

72. BA, Reg. 131, p. 4, Reg. 132, p. 2.

CHAPTER V: CRIMINAL JUSTICE

1. For a survey of criminal law and regulations according to the *Sharīᶜah*, see ᶜAbd al-Khāliq al-Nawāwī, *Jarā'im al-Jarḥ wa al-Ḍarb bayn al-Sharīᶜah wa al-Qānūn* (Cairo, 1970); Maydani Riyad, "ᶜUqūbāt: Penal Law," in *Law*, ed. Khadduri, pp. 223-35; Schacht, *Introduction*, pp. 175-98; and Tyan, "Judicial Organization," pp. 236-78.

2. BF, Reg. 120, Docs. 75, 79, 94, 106, 120, 202, 257, 309, 340, 352, 399, 503, and 543.

3. Al-Mawārdī, *Al-Aḥkām al-sulṭāniyyah* (Cairo, 1881), pp. 208, 212; Omar A. Farrukh, *Ibn Taimiyya on Public and Private Law in Islam* (Beirut, 1966), pp. 73-74; Heyd, *Ottoman Criminal Law*, pp. 241-44; and Tyan, "Judicial Organization," pp. 259-63.

4. The *multazim* collected taxes, supervised the cultivation of land by the peasants, and made sure that no land was left fallow. Shaw, *Financial Administration*, pp. 52-55; and ᶜAbd al-Raḥīm, *al-Rīf al-Miṣrī*, pp. 67-124.

5. BF, Reg. 120, Docs. 75, 106, 257, and 503; BA, Reg. 114, Doc. 175, Reg. 119, Docs. 557 and 1505, Reg. 123, Docs. 448, 1210, 1223, 1243, 1417, and 1489, Reg. 124, Doc. 65, and Reg. 126, Doc. 10.

6. Chapters V and VI.
7. BA, Reg. 125, Docs. 70, 187, and 414.
8. BA, Reg. 123, Doc. 1443.
9. BA, Reg. 125, Doc. 283.
10. BA, Reg. 121, Doc. 206, Reg. 123, Doc. 1516, Reg. 125, Docs. 701 and 987.
11. QA, Reg. 43.
12. BS, Reg. 134, Doc. 10; SA, Reg. 361, p. 2.
13. Occasionally a case was presented to the *qāḍī* in a petition, but usually nothing was said about petitions; the registers simply stated that this person had accused that person, BA, Reg. 123, Doc. 1243. Lane, who visited Egyptian courts in the nineteenth century, claimed that litigants first stated their cases to an *ᶜudūl*, who committed it to writing. Afterwards, the litigants went to the *qāḍī* for trial. Edward W. Lane, *An Account of the Manners and Customs of the Modern Egyptians* (New York, 1973), pp. 110-14.
14. BA, Reg. 125, Doc. 701.
15. BF, Reg. 120, Doc. 340.
16. BF, Reg. 120, Doc. 70; MQ, Reg. 101, Doc. 3.
17. BA, Reg. 124, Doc. 1215, Reg. 125, Doc. 110; BF, Reg. 120, Doc. 340.
18. BF, Reg. 120, Doc. 543; BA, Reg. 125, Doc. 283.
19. BF, Reg. 120, Doc. 70; MQ, Reg. 101, Doc. 3.
20. BA, Reg. 124, Doc. 196.
21. MQ, Reg. 101, Doc. 3.
22. BF, Reg. 120, Doc. 347.
23. BA, Reg. 125, Doc. 701.
24. BA, Reg. 125, Doc. 701.
25. BF, Reg. 120.
26. *Ibid.*
27. BA, Reg. 124, Doc. 215, Reg. 125, Doc. 701, Reg. 127, Doc. 1002.
28. BA, Reg. 124, Doc. 215.
29. BA, Reg. 123, Doc. 1223.
30. BA, Reg. 123, Doc. 1417.
31. BA, Reg. 122, Doc. 2145.
32. BF, Reg. 120, Doc. 543.
33. *Ibid.*
34. Coulson, pp. 124-27; and Heyd, *Ottoman Criminal Law*, pp. 244-27.
35. BA, Reg. 124, Doc. 65 (1055 A.H./1645 A.D.). For the views of jurists on fornication and false accusation of fornication, see Yaᶜqūb b. Abū Yūsuf, *Kitāb al-Kharāj* (Cairo, 1962), pp. 149-78.
36. QR, Reg. 47, p. 1 (1068 A.H./1658 A.D.)
37. For the views of the jurists on apostasy, see Abū Yūsuf, pp. 179-85.
38. BA, Reg. 121, Doc. 206 (1051 A.H./1641 A.D.).
39. Coulson, pp. 126-27.
40. BA, Reg. 125, Doc. 283 (1057 A.H./1647 A.D.).
41. BA, Reg. 125, Doc. 712 (1057 A.H./1647 A.D.).
42. BF, Reg. 120, Doc. 186 (1049 A.H./1634 A.D.).
43. BA, Reg. 181, Doc. 142 (1108 A.H./1696 A.D.).

44. BA, Reg. 124, Doc. 795 (1015 A.H./1606 A.D.).
45. BA, Reg. 123, Doc. 1443.
46. *Ibid.*
47. BF, Reg. 120, Doc. 75.
48. BA, Reg. 123, Doc. 1808.
49. BA, Reg. 123, Doc. 1243 (1056 A.H./1646 A.D.).
50. BA, Reg. 125, Doc. 1123.
51. *Ibid.*
52. BA, Reg. 123, Doc. 1017 (1056 A.H./1646 A.D.).
53. BA, Reg. 121, Doc. 336 (1053 A.H./1643 A.D.).
54. Coulson, pp. 125-27; Madkūr, *al-Qaḍa'*, pp. 83-84.
55. BA, Reg. 123, Doc. 893.
56. BA, Reg. 125, Doc. 70.
57. Al-Mawārdī, *Adab al-Qāḍī*, 2 vols. (Baghdad, 1972), 2:245-64.
58. BF, Reg. 120, Docs. 120, 207, and 211.
59. BA, Reg. 125, Docs. 109 and 719; BF, Reg. 120, Doc. 358.
60. BA, Reg. 123, Doc. 1903; BA, Reg. 124, Reg. 30.
61. BA, Reg. 123, Doc. 1243.
62. BA, Reg. 124, Doc. 101; BA, Reg. 128, Doc. 1876.
63. BA, Reg. 123, Doc. 1017.
64. Heyd, *Ottoman Criminal Law*, pp. 254-57.
65. BA, Reg. 123, Docs. 1223 and 1417.
66. Heyd, *Ottoman Criminal Law*, p. 243.
67. BF, Reg. 120, Doc. 552.
68. Heyd, *Ottoman Criminal Law*, p. 130.
69. BF, Reg. 120, Doc. 207.
70. BF, Reg. 120, Doc. 106.
71. BA, Reg. 125, Doc. 70.
72. *Ibid.*
73. BA, Reg. 181, Doc. 142.
74. BA, Reg. 123, Doc. 1849.
75. Heyd, *Ottoman Criminal Law*, pp. 221-22.
76. Raymond, "al-Qāhirah al-ᶜUthmāniyyah," pp. 232-33.
77. BA, Reg. 182, Doc. 141.
78. Heyd, *Ottoman Criminal Law*, p. 223.
79. *Ibid.*, p. 156.
80. BA, Reg. 123, Doc. 1648.
81. Heyd, *Ottoman Criminal Law*, p. 180.
82. *Ibid.*, p. 182.
83. BA, Reg. 117, Doc. 6.
84. BF, Reg. 20, Doc. ; BA, Reg. 122, Doc. 2111.
85. Heyd, *Ottoman Criminal Law*, pp. 219-21.
86. See Inalcik's review of Heyd's work in *BSOAS*, 37(1974):696-98.
87. BA, Reg. 119, Doc. 557.
88. BA, Reg. 121, Doc. 1516.
89. BA, Reg. 129, Doc. 1351.
90. There were two *dīwāns* in Egypt: *al-Dīwān al-ᶜĀlī* (the high council) was presided over by the *wālī* and included the heads of the military regiments and the treasury, the four *muftīs* and the *qāḍī ᶜaskar*. The principal executive and legislative council in Ottoman Egypt, it met three times every week. The smaller council was known simply as the *Dīwān*; it met every day. It was presided over by the lieutenant of the viceroy, the treasurer, and a *qāḍī*

known as the *qāḍī* of the *Dīwān*. See Shaw, *Financial Administration*, p. 2; al-Muwaylḥī, pp. 227-30.

91. BA, Reg. 123, Doc. 1849.
92. BA, Reg. 119, Doc. 1504, Reg. 123, Doc. 1086.
93. BA, Reg. 122, Doc. 1029.

CHAPTER VI: CIVIL CASES

1. For a survey of the civil law according to the *Sharī^{c}ah*, see ^{c}Abd al-Raḥman al-Jazīrī, *Kitāb al-Fiqh ^{c}alā al-Maẕāhib al-Arba^{c}ah*, 3 vols. (Cairo, n.d., 2-3; and Ṣubḥī Maḥamaṣānī, "Transactions in the Sharī^{c}ah," in *Law*, ed. Khadduri, pp. 179-202.
2. BF, Reg. 120, Docs. 287, 288, 293, and 297.
3. BF, Reg. 120, Docs. 147, 150, and 179.
4. BF, Reg. 120, Doc. 280.
5. BA, Reg. 124, Doc. 76 (1054 A.H./1644 A.D.).
6. BA, Reg. 127, Doc. 1003 (1059 A.H./1649 A.D.).
7. BA, Reg. 123, Doc. 1850 (1057 A.H./1647 A.D.).
8. BA, Reg. 125, Doc. 634 (1057 A.H./1647 A.D.).
9. BF, Reg. 120, Doc. 284.
10. *Ibid.*
11. BA, Reg. 128, Doc. 1894 (1061 A.H./1651 A.D.).
12. BA, Reg. 123, Doc. 1456 (1056 A.H./1646 A.D.).
13. BA, Reg. 123, Doc. 1802 (1057 A.H./1647 A.D.).
14. BA, Reg. 123, Doc. 1403 (1056 A.H./1646 A.D.).
15. BA, Reg. 127, Doc. 1084 (1059 A.H./1649 A.D.).
16. BA, Reg. 154, Doc. 487.
17. BA, Reg. 128, Doc. 322.
18. BA, Reg. 126, Doc. 53 (1058 A.H./1648 A.D.).
19. BA, Reg. 123, Doc. 1557 (1056 A.H./1646 A.D.). For similar cases, see also BA, Reg. 128, Doc. 1833.
20. BA, Reg. 126, Doc. no. not clear (1058 A.H./1648 A.D.).
21. Choucri Cardahi, "Conflict of Law," in *Law*, ed. Khadduri, p. 338.
22. BA, Reg. 123, Doc. 754.
23. BA, Reg. 119, Doc. 546, Reg. 129, Doc. 1351.
24. BA, Reg. 126, Doc. not clear.
25. BA, Reg. 123, Doc. 1444.
26. BA, Reg. 122, Doc. 1381.
27. BF, Reg. 120, Doc. 361.
28. Heyd, *Ottoman Criminal Law*, p. 129.
29. BA, Reg. 126, Doc. 894.
30. BA, Reg. 124, Docs. 35 and 95.
31. BA, Reg. 123, Doc. 1778.
32. BA, Reg. 111, p. 1.
33. *Ibid.*
34. BA, Reg. 123, Docs. 1478, 1557, and 1660.
35. BA, Reg. 121, Doc. 116, Reg. 123, Docs. 1478 and 1557, Reg. 126, Doc. 895.
36. BA, Reg. 124, Doc. 30.
37. *EI*^{2}, s.v. "Ḥiyal," by J. Schacht.
38. Jeanette Wakin, *The Functions of Documents in Islamic Law* (Albany, 1972), pp. 29-37.

39. *EI*[2], s.v. "Ribā," by J. Schacht; Fazlur Rahman, "Ribā and Interest," *SI* 3(1964):1-43.
40. Heyd, *Ottoman Criminal Law*, p. 122.
41. For the practice of interest in the Ottoman Empire, see Naṣ'et Çağatay, "Ribā and Interest Concept and Banking in the Ottoman Empire," *SI* 32(1970):53-68.
42. BA, Reg. 126, Doc. 182.
43. Cf. Coulson, p. 139.
44. Cardahi, pp. 334-41.
45. *Ibid.*
46. BA, Reg. 126, Doc. 9.
47. BA, Reg. 119, Doc. 415, Reg. 123, Docs. 291 and 1451, Reg. 124, Doc. 200, Reg. 125, Docs. 148, 499, and 638, Reg. 126, Doc. 175. For *awqāf* established by non-Muslims, see Chapter IX; for social status of non-Muslims, see Chapter VIII.
48. Madkūr, *al-Qaḍā'*, p. 86.
49. Al-Nawāwī, pp. 64-75.
50. *Ibid.*

CHAPTER VII: FAMILY LAW

1. For a survey of family law and the status of women and non-Muslims according to the *Sharīᶜah*, see al-Jazīrī, *al-Fiqh*, vol. 4; Muḥammad Abū Zahra, "Family Law," in *Law*, ed. Khadduri, pp. 132-78; Schacht, *Introduction*, pp. 161-74; Gibb and Bowen, 2:207, 262; and Cardahi, pp. 334-48.
2. BA, Reg. 121, Doc. 14, Reg. 123, Doc. 752, Reg. 126, Docs. 39 and 878, Reg. 127, Doc. 646, and Reg. 181, Doc. 143.
3. BA, Reg. 119, Doc. 515 (1048 A.H./1638 A.D.).
4. BA, Reg. 125, Doc. 1153 (1058 A.H./1648 A.D.).
5. BA, Reg. 119, Doc. 1866, Reg. 124, Doc. 5.
6. *Ibid.*
7. BA, Reg. 123, Doc. 752, Reg. 127, Doc. 646.
8. BA, Reg. 121, Docs. 14 and 236, Reg. 124, Doc. 1131, Reg. 126, Doc. 89.
9. BA, Reg. 119, Doc. 2288, Reg. 123, Doc. 1803, Reg. 124, Doc. 1102.
10. BA, Reg. 123, Doc. 1367.
11. *Ibid.*
12. BA, Reg. 127, Doc. 413 (1059 A.H./1649 A.D.).
13. Coulson, p. 97.
14. BA, Reg. 121, Docs. 29 and 336, Reg. 124, Docs. 370, 834, and 1131.
15. BA, Reg. 119, Doc. 666, Reg. 124, Doc. 1131.
16. BA, Reg. 119, Doc. 586.
17. BA, Reg. 124, Doc. 559 (1054 A.H./1644 A.D.).
18. BA, Reg. 123, Doc. 1770 (1057 A.H./1647 A.D.).
19. BA, Reg. 154, Doc. 398 (1082 A.H./1671 A.D.).
20. BA, Reg. 127, Doc. 725.
21. Coulson, p. 97.
22. *Ibid.*
23. BA, Reg. 121, Docs. 14 and 45, Reg. 126, Doc. 878, Reg. 127, Doc. 646, Reg. 179, Doc. 45.

24. Abu Zahra, pp. 140-41.
25. *Ibid.*
26. BA, Reg. 126, Doc. 909 (1058 A.H./1648 A.D.). For similar cases, see BA, Reg. 121, Docs. 66, 458, and 459, Reg. 122, Docs. 164 and 604, Reg. 123, Doc. 1161, Reg. 124, Docs. 12 and 1118, Reg. 125, Doc. 637.
27. For division of inheritance elsewhere in the Empire, see Barkan, *Edirne Askeri*; Orhanlu, "Ḳassām"; and H. Inalcik, "Documents on the Economic and Social History of Turkey in the 15th Century," *RFSEUI* 15-16(1953-55):44-48.
28. QR, Reg. 133, p. 1, Reg. 134, p. 1.
29. QA, Regs. 33, 34, 42, 47, and 51.
30. Shaw, *Financial Administration*, p. 171.
31. QA, Reg. 43, Doc. 98.
32. BF, Reg. 120, Doc. 208 (1049 A.H./1639 A.D.).
33. QA, Reg. 34, Doc. 458.
34. QA, Reg. 33, Doc. 12.
35. QA, Reg. 51, Doc. 918.
36. *Ibid.*
37. QA, Reg. 34, Doc. 27.
38. QA, Reg. 33, Docs. 12 and 31.
39. QA, Reg. 34, Doc. 27.
40. QA, Reg. 34, Doc. 41.
41. *Ibid.*
42. *Ibid.*
43. BA, Reg. 127, Doc. 1628 (1059 A.H./1649 A.D.).
44. BA, Reg. 126, Doc. 895 (1058 A.H./1648 A.D.).
45. Gibb and Bowen, 2:28.
46. QA, Reg. 51, Doc. 918.
47. QA, Reg. 43, Doc. 98.
48. QR, Reg. 55, Docs. 55, 156, 157, and 346.
49. QR, Reg. 55, Doc. 72, Reg. 74, Docs. 32 and 93.
50. *Ibid.*, Doc. 216.
51. BA, Reg. 125, Docs. 364-367.
52. *Ibid.*
53. According to Ottoman *qānūn*, the first 10,000 *niṣfs* was to go to the provincial governors (the *wālī*, in the case of Egypt), and the rest to the treasury. See Inalcik, "Bursa Şer^c^iye," pp. 699-700; and Shaw, *Financial Administration*, pp. 173-74. QA, Reg. 34, Doc. 458, Reg. 43, Doc. 98, Reg. 51, Doc. 918.
54. QR, Reg. 55, Docs. 54, 55, 71, 156, 157, and 346, Reg. 74, Docs. 41 and 42.
55. For the legal status of women elsewhere in the Ottoman Empire, see Jennings, pp. 245-83.
56. Morroe Berger, *The Arab World Today* (New York, 1962), pp. 117-40; and Reuben Levy, *The Social Structure of Islam* (Cambridge, 1957), pp. 91-134.
57. BA, Reg. 121, Docs. 66, 458, and 459, Reg. 122, Docs. 164 and 604.
58. BF, Reg. 120, Doc. 280.
59. BA, Reg. 121, Doc. 302.
60. BF, Reg. 120, Docs. 180 and 504.
61. BA, Reg. 126, Doc. 409.

62. BA, Reg. 124, Doc. 170, Reg. 127, Doc. 646.
63. BA, Reg. 119, Doc. 335.
64. BF, Reg. 120, Docs. 14, 15, 20, 44, 48, 55, 131, and 137.
65. BF, Reg. 120, Doc. 148.
66. Abu Zahra, p. 160.
67. BF, Reg. 120, Docs. 14, 15, 20, 44, 48, 55, 131, 137, 147, 150, 179, and 194.

CHAPTER VIII: THE ROLE OF THE COURT IN URBAN ADMINISTRATION

1. BF, Reg. 120, Docs. 456, 482, 496, and 497; BA, Reg. 121, Docs. 93, 124, 665, and 666, and Reg. 126, Docs. 19, 45, 51, 53, 216, and 325.
2. According to one survey, the military during the seventeenth century accounted for about 90 per cent of the *multazims* in Egypt. The other 8 per cent included ulema, heads of Arab tribes, and merchants. ᶜAbd al-Raḥīm, *Al-Rīf al-Miṣrī*, p. 88.
3. Inalcik, *The Ottoman Empire*, p. 69.
4. BA, Reg. 154. The number of the document and the page is not clear.
5. BF, Reg. 120, Doc. 335.
6. BF, Reg. 120, Doc. 510.
7. Lapidus, pp. 85-95; Raymond, "Al-Qāhirah al-ᶜUthmāniyyah," pp. 216-25. For other Ottoman cities, see *EI*^{2}, s.v. "Istanbul," by Halil Inalcik.
8. Levy, p. 337.
9. BA, Reg. 125, Doc. 236.
10. QS, Reg. 130, Doc. 19.
11. BF, Reg. 120, Doc. 46.
12. BA, Reg. 124, Doc. 785.
13. BA, Reg. 125, Doc. 245.
14. BA, Reg. 122, Doc. 1051.
15. BA, Reg. 126, Doc. 270.
16. BA, Reg. 124, Doc. 200, Reg. 127, Doc. 1744.
17. BA, Reg. 124, Doc. 200.
18. *Ibid.*
19. BA, Reg. 127, Doc. 1744 (1060 A.H./1650 A.D.).
20. For the social makeup of the *ḥārah* in Cairo, see Raymond, "Al-Qāhirah al-ᶜUthmāniyyah," pp. 216-25; "Al-Aḥyā' al-Aristuqrāṭiyyah bī al-Qāhirah fī al-Qarn al-Thāmin ᶜAshar," trans. Zuhayr al-Shāyib, *al-Majallah*, 149(1969):69-86; "Aḥyā'al-Qāhirah al-Shaᶜbiyyah fī al-Qarn al-Thāmin ᶜAshar wa al-Harakāt al-Jamāhīriyyah al-Lattī Qāmat Bihā," trans. Zuhayr al-Shāyib, *Al-Talīᶜah* 7(1968)46-54. For the social organization of other Ottoman cities, see Inalcik, "Istanbul."
21. BA, Reg. 127, Docs. 1002 and 1632.
22. BA, Reg. 127, Doc. 1002.
23. BA, Reg. 122, Doc. 340.
24. In the nineteenth century E. Lane had to move out of a neighborhood in Cairo simply because the families and married people resented having a single man among them; Lane, p. 155.

25. BA, Reg. 122, Doc. 340.
26. BA, Reg. 125, Doc. 701.
27. BA, Reg. 124, Doc. 213.
28. QS, Reg. 120, Doc. 148.
29. BA, Reg. 126, Doc. 667.
30. QS, Reg. 130, Doc. 19.
31. BA, Reg. 122, Doc. 1511.
32. QS, Reg. 130, Docs. 19 and 148; BA, Reg. 125, Doc. 245, Reg. 127, Doc. 1002.
33. *Ibid.*
34. QS, Reg. 130, Doc. 138.
35. BA, Reg. 125, Doc. 245.
36. BA, Reg. 124, Docs. 785 and 786.
37. The practice of admitting non-Muslims into Muslim courts in the mosques began long before the Ottoman era in Egypt. See Muḥammad b. Yūsuf al-Kindī, *The History of the Egyptian Kadis*, ed. Richard J.H. Gottheil (London, 1908), pp. 74-76.
38. BA, Reg. 123, Doc. 1636, Reg. 125, Doc. 215.
39. BA, Reg. 123, Doc. 1812, Reg. 127, Doc. 1084.
40. BA, Reg. 125, Doc. 1152.
41. BA, Reg. 121, Doc. 182, Reg. 124, Doc. 14, Reg. 127, Doc. 1084.
42. BF, Reg. 120, Doc. 2.
43. BA, Reg. 125, Docs. 506 and 667.
44. For the legal status of non-Muslims, see above, pp. 42-43; see also Abū Yūsuf, pp. 127-28; and I. Lichtenstadter, "The Distinctive Dress of Non-Muslims in Islamic Countries," *HJ* 5(1943): 35-52.
45. BA, Reg. 127, Doc. 1632.
46. SA, Reg. 317, p. 1.
47. BA, Reg. 127, Doc. 400.
48. BA, Reg. 120, Doc. 206.
49. BA, Reg. 126, Doc. 9.
50. For the economic organization of other Ottoman cities, see Inalcik, "Istanbul," "Ottoman Economic Mind," pp. 205-18, "Capital Formation," pp. 97-140, and *The Ottoman Empire*, pp. 140-61.
51. For a detailed list of guilds in Egypt, see Baer, *Egyptian Guilds*, pp. 166-76; and André Raymond, "Une liste des corporations des métiers au Caire en 1801," *Arabica*, 4(1957):151-63.
52. BA, Reg. 119, Docs. 125 and 883, Reg. 121, Docs. 33, 543, 552, 747, and 811, Reg. 122, Docs. 16, 17, 67, 483, 514, 1078, 1304, 1379, and 1515, Reg. 123, Docs. 100, 109, 958, 970, 1116, 1155, and 1442, Reg. 128, Doc. 1936, 1940, 1946, and 1587.
53. BA, Reg. 122, Doc. 67, Reg. 128, Doc. 932.
54. BA, Reg. 122, Doc. 1078.
55. BA, Reg. 128, Doc. 1177.
56. BA, Reg. 122, Doc. 67.
57. BA, Reg. 127, Doc. 1645.
58. BA, Reg. 121, Doc. 33, Reg. 128, Doc. 1936.
59. BA, Reg. 121, Doc. 747 (1053 A.H./1643 A.D.).
60. BA, Reg. 125, Doc. 1110 (1057 A.H./1647 A.D.).
61. BA, Reg. 127, Doc. 1684.
62. BA, Reg. 122, Doc. 17 (1052 A.H./1642 A.D.).

63. BA, Reg. 122, Doc. 1379 (1051 A.H./1641 A.D.).
64. BA, Reg. 125, Doc. 399 (1057 A.H./1647 A.D.).
65. BA, Reg. 119, Docs. 123 and 883, Reg. 121, Docs. 33, 552, 747, and 827, Reg. 122, Docs. 16, 17, 514, 1379, and 1515, Reg. 124, Doc. 414, Reg. 125, Docs. 216, 399, and 1110, Reg. 128, Docs. 1587, 1936, 1940, and 1946.
66. BA, Reg. 121, Doc. 33.
67. BA, Reg. 127, Doc. 1482.
68. BA, Reg. 121, Doc. 747, Reg. 128, Doc. 1436.
69. BA, Reg. 122, Doc. 67.
70. For the organization of the guilds in Istanbul, see Inalcik, *The Ottoman Empire*, pp. 150-61, "Economic Mind," pp. 215-16, and "Capital Formation," pp. 130-40.
71. BA, Reg. 122, Doc. 1813.
72. BA, Reg. 126, Doc. 8.
73. BA, Reg. 125, Doc. 1011.
74. BA, Reg. 123, Doc. 970.
75. BA, Reg. 121, Doc. 33.
76. BA, Reg. 125, Doc. 399.
77. BF, Reg. 120, Doc. 308.
78. BA, Reg. 121, Doc. 747.
79. BA, Reg. 125, Doc. 1169.
80. BA, Reg. 124, Doc. 1442.
81. BA, Reg. 128, Doc. 1177.
82. BA, Reg. 123, Doc. 33.
83. *Ibid.*
84. BA, Reg. 122, Doc. 1894.
85. Terence Walz, "Wakalat al-Gallaba: The Market for Sudan Goods in Cairo," *Annales*, 13(1977):217-45.
86. *Ibid.*
87. Inalcik, *The Ottoman Empire*, pp. 150-56, "Economic Mind," pp. 215-18, and "Capital Formation," pp. 120-40.
88. BA, Reg. 122, Doc. 67.
89. SA, Reg. 316, p. 2.
90. BA, Reg. 122, Doc. 1078.
91. BA, Reg. 123, Doc. 68, Reg. 127, Doc. 1648.
92. BA, Reg. 122, Doc. 1078 (1051 A.H./1641 A.D.).
93. The *raṭl* was 1 lb. 2 oz. 5-3/4 dwt. to about 1 lb. 2 oz. 8 dwt. The *dirham* was 47-5/8 to 48 English grams. Lane, p. 572.
94. BA, Reg. 127, Doc. 1358 (1059 A.H./1649 A.D.).
95. BA, Reg. 127, Doc. 424.
96. BA, Reg. 125, Doc. 64 (1057 A.H./1647 A.D.).
97. BA, Reg. 123, Doc. 100 (1056 A.H./1646 A.D.).
98. BA, Reg. 124, Doc. 1442 (1055 A.H./1645 A.D.).
99. BA, Reg. 123, Doc. 1813 (1057 A.H./1647 A.D.).

CHAPTER IX: RURAL ADMINISTRATION AND THE ADMINISTRATION OF THE AWQĀF

1. Al-Muwaylḥī, pp. 244-45.
2. For the rural administration of Ottoman Egypt, see ᶜAbd al-Raḥīm, *al-Rīf al-Miṣrī*, pp. 1-63; Shaw, *Financial Administration*, pp. 60-61; and al-Muwaylḥī, pp. 224-58.

3. Mubārak, *al-Khiṭaṭ*, 16:88-89.
4. BF, Reg. 120, Doc. 107.
5. BF, Reg. 120, Docs. 187 and 199.
6. BF, Reg. 120, Docs. 88 and 89.
7. BF, Reg. 120, Doc. 335.
8. ᶜAbd al-Raḥīm, *al-Rīf al-Miṣrī*, pp. 285-87; Shaw, *Financial Administration*, pp. 227-28.
9. *Ibid.*
10. ᶜAbd al-Raḥīm, *al-Rīf al-Miṣrī*, pp. 285-87.
11. BF, Reg. 120, Doc. 12.
12. BF, Reg. 120, Docs. 501 and 502.
13. BF, Reg. 120, Doc. 292.
14. Shaw, *Financial Administration*, pp. 64-97.
15. BF, Reg. 120, Doc. 519.
16. BF, Reg. 120, Doc. 178.
17. BF, Reg. 120, Doc.
18. BF, Reg. 120, Doc. 132.
19. BF, Reg. 120, Doc. 71 (1048 A.H./1638 A.D.).
20. BF, Reg. 120, Doc. 178.
21. BF, Reg. 120, Doc. 335 (1050 A.H./1640 A.D.).
22. BF, Reg. 120, Doc. 183 (1049 A.H./1639 A.D.).
23. Gibb and Bowen, 1:172-73; Shaw, *Financial Administration*, pp. 41-50, and "Land Law, pp. 106-38.
24. *Ibid.*
25. Shaw, *Financial Administration*, p. 43.
26. *Ibid.*
27. *Ibid.*
28. For a survey of the *awqāf* established by the viceroy of Egypt and other members of the ruling class, see John Alden Williams, "The Monuments of Ottoman Cairo," *Colloque International sur l'Histoire du Caire* (Cairo: Ministry of Culture, 1972), pp. 453-63; and Raymond, "Al-Qāhirah al-ᶜUthmāniyyah," pp. 250-53.
29. BA, Reg. 123, Doc. 1270, Reg. 127, Docs. 175, 428, and 779.
30. BF, Reg. 120, Doc. 148; BA, Reg. 123, Doc. 1451, Reg. 125, Doc. 622.
31. BA, Reg. 119, Doc. 151.
32. BA, Reg. 119, Doc. 7.
33. *Ibid.*
34. BA, Reg. 139, Doc. no. unclear.
35. BF, Reg. 120, Doc. 308.
36. BA, Reg. 123, Doc. 1451, Reg. 124, Doc. 200, Reg. 125, Docs. 148, 499, and 638.
37. BA, Reg. 119, Doc. 1030.
38. BA, Reg. 139, Doc. 300.
39. BA, Reg. 119, Doc. 1030.
40. BA, Reg. 126, Doc. 880-883.
41. *Ibid.*
42. BA, Reg. 121, Docs. 18, 27-29, 40, 46-50, 70, and 291.
43. BA, Reg. 119, Doc. 585.
44. *Ibid.*
45. BA, Reg. 122, Doc. 2208.
46. BA, Reg. 139, Doc. 310.
47. BA, Reg. 119, Doc. 585.

48. BA, Reg. 122, Doc. 760.
49. BA, Reg. 165, p. 3.
50. BA, Reg. 128, Doc. 1089.
51. BA, Reg. 126, Docs. 1076-1080.

APPENDIX A

1. For information on other courts which supposedly existed in Cairo, but from which no registers exist today, see Chapter III.

2. The dates shown are the dates of the first and last registers of the courts. The courts of Būlāq, Miṣr al-Qadīmah, al-Ṣāliḥiyyah, al-Ṣāliḥ, al-Ḥākim, and Ṭūlūn pre-date the Ottoman era, but no pre-Ottoman registers from any of the courts are known to exist. Mīlād, pp. 82-137.

3. For location of the mosques and schools, see Mubārak, vols. 1-3.

4. For information on the location of the courts, see Ramzī , vols. 1-5.

APPENDIX B

1. The ranking system was based on the revenue of the courts with the highest revenue-producing courts ranking highest. Mubārak, 14:88-89; [c]Abd al-Raḥīm, *Al-Rīf al-Miṣrī*, p. 41; Bachatly, pp. 1-18; and Shaw, *Ottoman Egypt*, p. 96.

APPENDIX C

1. The registers listed do not include other specialized registers which were used by the court during the eighteenth century; see Chapter II.

BIBLIOGRAPHY

ARCHIVAL MATERIALS

The Court	*The Registers*
Al-Bāb al-ᶜĀlī	106, 107, 111, 112, 113, 114, 115, 116, 117, 119, 121, 122, 123, 124, 125, 126, 127, 128, 129, 131, 132, 133, 136, 139, 140, 141, 142, 143, 145, 149, 151, 152, 153, 157, 161, 163, 164, 166, 167, 173, 179, 180
Al-Qismah al-ᶜAskariyyah	55, 60, 62, 74, 133, 134, 135, 136, 137, 138, 144
Al-Qismah al-ᶜArabiyyah	33, 34, 42, 43, 47, 51
Būlāq	36, 51, 52, 54, 60
Miṣr al-Qadīmah	98, 101
Qanāṭir al-Sibāᶜ	126, 130, 133, 144, 147
Ṭūlūn	194, 196
Qūṣūn	246, 259
Al-Ṣāliḥ	316, 317, 340, 361
Bāb al-Saᶜādah	424
Al-Ṣāliḥiyyah	479, 516, 526
Bāb al-Shaᶜriyyah	629, 634
Al-Barmashiyyah	710, 711

MANUSCRIPTS

Al-Bakrī, Muḥammad b. Abī al-Surūr. "Al-Kawākib al-Sā'irah fī Akhbār Miṣr wa al-Qāhirah." London: British Library, MS. Add. 7324.

________. "Al-Tuḥfah al-Bahiyyah fī Tamaluk Āl ᶜUthmān al-Diyār al-Miṣriyyah." Vienna: National Bibliothek, MS. A.F. 283.

Al-Maddāḥ, Muṣṭafā b. Ibrāhīm. "Majmūᶜ Laṭīf." Vienna: National Bibliothek, MS. Arabe 931, H.O. 38.

GENERAL WORKS

Abbas, Ihsan. *ᶜAhd Ardshir*. Beirut: Dār Ṣādir, 1967.

ᶜAbd al-Raḥīm, ᶜAbd al-Raḥīm A. *Al-Rīf al-Miṣrī fī al-Qarn al-Thāmin ᶜAshar*. Cairo: Maṭbaᶜat ᶜAyn Shams, 1974.

__________. "Al-Qaḍā' fī Miṣr al-^{c}Uthmāniyyah." In *Buḥūth fī al-Tārīkh al-Ḥadīth*. Cairo: Egyptian Historical Society, 1976.

Abu-Lughod, Janel L. *Cairo: 1001 Years of the City Victorious*. Princeton: Princeton University Press, 1971.

Abū Yūsuf, Ya^{c}qūb. *Kitāb al-Kharāj*. Cairo: al-Maṭba^{c}ah al-Salafiyyah, 1962.

Abu Zahra, Muhammad. "Family Law." In *Law in the Middle East*, ed. M. Khadduri and H.J. Liebesny, pp. 132-78. Washington: Middle East Institute, 1955.

Anīs, Muḥammad. *Madrasat al-Tārīkh al-Miṣrī fī al-^{c}Aṣr al-Uthmānī*. Cairo: Ma^{c}had al-Dirāsāt al-^{c}Arabiyyah, 1962.

^{c}Arnūs, Maḥmūd b. *Tārīkh al-Qaḍā' fī al-Islām*. Cairo: n.p., 1934.

^{c}Āshūr, Sa^{c}īd. *Al-^{c}Aṣr al-Mamālīkī fī Miṣr wa al-Shām*. Cairo: Dār al-Nahḍah, 1965.

__________. *Al-Mujtama^{c} al-Miṣrī fī ^{c}Aṣr Salaṭin al-Mamālīk*. Cairo: Dār al-Naḥdah, 1962.

__________. "Al-Fallāḥ wa al-Iqṭā^{c} fī ^{c}Aṣr al-Ayyūbiyīn wa al-Mamālīk." In *Al-Arḍ wa al-Fallāḥ fī Miṣr ^{c}alā Marr al-^{c}Uṣūr*, pp. 210-24. Cairo: Egyptian Historical Society, 1974.

Al-^{c}Asqalānī, Aḥmad b. Hajar. *Raf^{c} al-Iṣr ^{c}an Quḍāt Miṣr*. Cairo: Ministry of Education, 1957.

Ayalon, David. "The Great Yāsa of Chingiz Khān: A Re-Examination." *Studia Islamica* 38(1973):110-27.

Bachatly, C.A. "L'Administration de la justice en Egypte à la veille des reformes de l'an IX, d'après un document arabe inédit." *Bulletin de l'Institut Egyptien* 18 (1935):1-18.

Baer, Gabriel. *Egyptian Guilds in Modern Times*. Jerusalem: Israel Oriental Society, 1964.

__________. *Studies in the Social History of Modern Egypt*. Chicago: University of Chicago Press, 1969.

Barkan, Ö.L. *XV ve XVI-Inci Asirlarda Osmanli Imparatorlugunda Zirai Ekonominin Hukukî ve Malî Esaslari - Kānūnlar*. Istanbul: Burhaneddin Matbaasi, 1945.

__________. "Edirne Askerî Kassamina âit Tereke Defterler, 1545-1659." *Belgeler* 3(1966):1-479.

Berger, Morroe. *The Arab World Today*. New York: Doubleday, 1962.

Catagay, Nas'et. "Ribā and Interest Concept and Banking in the Ottoman Empire." *Studia Islamica* 32(1970):53-68.

Cahen, Claude. "A propos de Shuhud." *Studia Islamica* 31(1970):71-79.

Cardahi, Choucri. "Conflict of Law." In *Law in the Middle East*, ed. M. Khadduri and H.J. Liebesny. Washington: Middle East Institute, 1955.

Chattan, H. "The Law of Wakf." In *Law in the Middle East*, ed. M. Khadduri and H.J. Liebesny. Washington: Middle East Institute, 1955.

Coulson, N.H. *A History of Islamic Law*. Edinburgh: University Press, 1964.

Crecelius, Daniel. "The Organization of Waqf Documents in Cairo." *International Journal of Middle East Studies* 2(1971):266-77.

Darrag, Ahmad. *L'Egypte sous le règne de Barsbay, 825-841/1422-1438*. Damascus: Institut Français de Damas, 1961.

Darke, Hubert. *The Book of Government or Rules for Kings: The Siyar al-Muluk or Siyasat-nama of Nizam al-Mulk*. London: Routledge and Kegan Paul, 1960.

Encyclopedia of Islam, 2nd rev. ed. S.v. "Ḳānūn," by Linant de Bellefonds and Halil Inalcik.

__________. S.v. "Ḳānūnnāme," by Halil Inalcik.

__________. S.v. "Istiḥsān," by R. Paret.

__________. S.v. "Ḥājib," by E. Tyan.

__________. S.v. "Ḥisba," by Claude Cahen and M. Talbi.

__________. S.v. "Ḳassām," by Cengiz Orhanlu.

__________. S.v. "Istanbul," by Halil Inalcik.

__________. S.v. "Ribā," by J. Schacht

__________. S.v. "Ḥiyal," by J. Schacht.

Farrukh, Omar. *Ibn Taimiyya on Public and Private Law in Islam*. Beirut: Khayyāt, 1966.

Gibb, H.A.R., and Harold Bowen. *Islamic Society and the West: A Study of the Impact of Western Civilization on Muslim Culture in the Near East*. London: Oxford University Press, 1950-1957.

Heyd, Uriel. *Studies in Old Ottoman Criminal Law*, ed. V.L. Menage. Oxford: Oxford University Press, 1973.

__________. "Ḳānūn and Sharīᶜa in Old Ottoman Criminal Justice." *Proceedings of the Israel Academy of Sciences and Humanities* 3(1967):1-18.

__________. "Some Aspects of Ottoman Fetvā." *Bulletin of the School of Oriental and African Studies* 32(1969):35-56.

Hinz, W. *Islamische Masse und Gewichte umgerechnet ins metrische System*. Leiden: Brill, 1955.

Holt, P.M., ed. *Political and Social Change in Modern Egypt*. London: Oxford University Press, 1968.

__________. *Egypt and the Fertile Crescent, 1516-1922: A Political History*. New York: Cornell University Press, 1966.

__________. "The Pattern of Egyptian Political History from 1517 to 1798." In *Political and Social Change in Modern Egypt*, ed. P.M. Holt, pp. 91-103. London: Oxford University Press, 1968.

__________. "Ottoman Egypt (1517-1798): An Account of Arabic Historical Sources." In *Political and Social Change in Modern Egypt*, ed. P.M. Holt, pp. 28-51. London: Oxford University Press, 1968.

Ibn Taymiyyah, Aḥmad. *Al-Siyāsah al-Sharᶜiyyah fī Iṣlāh al-Rāᶜī wa al-Raᶜiyyah*, ed. ᶜAlī Sāmī al-Nushar and Aḥmad Zakī. Cairo: Dār al-Kitāb, 1951.

Inalcik, Halil. *The Ottoman Empire: The Classical Age, 1300-1600*. Translated by Norman Itzkowitz and Colin Imber. New York: Praeger, 1973.

__________. "The Ottoman Economic Mind and Aspects of the Ottoman Economy." In *Studies in the Economic History of the Middle East*, ed. M.A. Cook. London: Oxford University Press, 1970.

__________. "The Nature of Traditional Society--Turkey." In *Political Modernization in Japan and Turkey*, ed. R.E. Ward and Dankwart A. Rustow. Princeton: Princeton University Press, 1964.

__________. "Capital Formation in the Ottoman Empire." *Journal of Economic History* 29 (1969):97-140.

__________. "Ottoman Methods of Conquest." *Studia Islamica* 2(1954): 103-29.

Inalcik, Halil. "Bursa and the Commerce of the Levant." *Journal of Economic and Social History of the Orient* 3(1960):131-42.

__________. "Adâletnâ meler." *Turk Tarih Belgeleri Dergisi* 2(1967): 49-145.

__________. "Bursa Şer^ciye Sicillerinde Fatih Sultan Mehmed' in Fermanlari." *Belleten* 11(1947):693-703.

__________. "Documents on the Economic and Social History of Turkey in the 15th Century." *Revue de la Faculte des Sciences Economiques* (University of Istanbul) 15-16(1953-55):44-48.

__________. "Suleyman the Lawgiver and Ottoman Law." *Archivum Ottomanicum* 1(1969):105-38.

Islam Ansiklopedisi. S.v. "Örf," by Halil Inalcik.

Iyās, Ahmad b. *Bada'i^c al-Zuhūr fi Waqa'i^c al-Duhūr*. 5 vols. Cairo: Franz Steiner, 1961.

Al-Jabarti, ^{c}Abd al-Raḥman. *^{c}Ajā'ib al-Athar fī al-Tarājim wa al-Akhbār*. 7 vols. Cairo: Lajnat al-Bayān, 1958.

Al-Jazīrī, ^{c}Abd al-Raḥman. *Kitāb al-Fiqh ^{c}ala al-Maẕāhib al-Arba^{c}ah*. 3 vols. Cairo: al-Maktabah al-Tujāriyyaẖ, n.d.

Jennings, R., Jr. "The Judicial Registers (Şer^{c}i Mahkeme Sicilleri) of Kayseri." Ph.D. dissertation, University of Michigan, 1972.

__________. "Women in Early Seventeenth-Century Ottoman Judicial Records--The Sharia Court of Anatolian Kayseri." *Journal of the Economic and Social History of the Orient* 18(1975):53-114.

__________. "The Office of Vekīl (Wakīl) in Seventeenth-Century Ottoman Sharia Courts." *Studia Islamica* 42(1957):147-69.

Khadduri, Majid, and H.J. Liebesny, eds. *Law in the Middle East*. Washington: Middle East Institute, 1955.

Al-Kindī, Muḥammad b. Yūsuf. *The History of the Egyptian Kadis*, ed. Richard J.H. Gottheil. London: Luzac, 1908.

Lambton, A.K.S. "Justice in the Medieval Persian Theory of Kingship." *Studia Islamica* 17(1962):91-120.

Lane, Edward W. *An Account of the Manners and Customs of the Modern Egyptians*. New York: Dover Publications, 1973.

Lapidus, Ira M. *Muslim Cities in the Later Middle Ages*. Cambridge: Harvard University Press, 1967.

Levy, Reuben. *The Social Structure of Islam*. Cambridge: Cambridge University Press, 1967.

Lewis, Bernard. "The Islamic Guilds." *Economic History Review* 8 (1937-38):20-37.

__________. "Ottoman Observers of Ottoman Decline." *Islamic Studies* 1(1962):71-87.

Lichtenstadter, Ilse. "The Distinctive Dress of Non-Muslims in Islamic Countries." *Historia Judaica* 5(1943):35-52.

Madkūr, Muḥammad. *Aḥkām al-Usrah fī al-Islam*. 5 vols. Cairo: Dār al-Nahḍah, 1969-70.

__________. *Al-Qaḍā' fī al-Islam*. Cairo: Dar al-Nahḍah, 1964.

Mahmasani, Subhi. "Transactions in the Shari^{c}ah." In *Law in the Middle East*, ed. M. Khadduri and H.J. Liebesny, pp. 179-202. Washington: Middle East Institute, 1955.

Al-Maqrīzī, Taqiyy al-Dīn. *Al-Khitat al-Maqrīziyyah*. 2 vols. Baghdad: al-Muthannā, 1970.

Al-Mawārdī, ^{c}Alī b. Muḥammad. *Adab al-Qāḍī*, ed. Mohie H. al-Sarhān. 2 vols. Baghdad: Diwān al-Awqāf, 1971-1972.

Al-Mawārdī, ᶜAlī b. Muḥammad. *Al-Aḥkām al-Sulṭāniyyah.* Cairo: Maṭbaᶜat al-Waṭan, 1881.

Maydani, Riyad. "ᶜUqubat: Penal Law." In *Law in the Middle East*, ed. M. Khadduri and H.J. Liebesny, pp. 223-35. Washington: Middle East Institute, 1955.

Mubārak, ᶜAlī. *Al-Khiṭaṭ al-Tawfīqiyyah.* 4 vols. Cairo: Būlāq, 1886-1889.

Al-Muḥibbī, Muḥammad. *Khulāṣat al-Athar fī Aᶜyan al-Qarn al-Hādī ᶜAshar.* 5 vols. Beirut: Khayāṭ, 1966.

Al-Muwaylḥī, Ibraḥīm. "Al-Arḍ wa al-Fallāḥ fī al-ᶜAṣr al-ᶜUthmānī." In *Al-Arḍ wa al-Fallāḥ fī Miṣr ᶜalā Marr al-ᶜUṣūr*, pp. 224-58. Cairo: Egyptian Historical Society, 1974.

Al-Nawāwī, ᶜAbd al-Khāliq. *Jarā'im al-Jarḥ wa al-Ḍarb bayn al-Sharīᶜah wa al-Qānūn.* Cairo: Dār al-Fikr al-ᶜArabī, 1970.

Pixley, Michael M. "The Development and Role of the Şeyhülislam in Early Ottoman History." *Journal of the American Oriental Society* 96 (1976):4-44.

Polk, William R., and Richard L. Chambers, eds. *Beginnings of Modernization in the Middle East.* Chicago: University of Chicago Press, 1968.

Al-Qalqashandī, Aḥmad. *Ṣubh al-Aᶜshā fī Ṣinaᶜat al-Inshā.* 14 vols. Cairo: Ministry of Culture, n.d.

Al-Rāfᶜī, ᶜAbd al-Raḥman. *Tārīkh al-Ḥarakah al-Qawmiyyah.* 3 vols. Cairo: Maṭbaᶜat al-Nahḍah, 1929.

Rāfiq, ᶜAbd al-Karīm. *Bilād al-Shām wa Miṣr (1516-1798).* Damascus: n.p., 1968.

Rahman, Fazlur. "Ribā and Interest." *Islamic Studies* 3(1964):1-43.

Ramzī, Muḥammad. *Al-Qāmūs al-Jughrāfī.* 5 vols. Cairo: Dār al-Kutub, 1953-1963.

Al-Rāqid, Muḥammad A. *Al-Ghazw al-ᶜUthmanī li Miṣr.* Cairo: Mu'assasat al-Shabāb al-Jāmiᶜah, 1968.

Raymond, André. *Artisans et commerçants au Caire au XVIIIe siècle.* 2 vols. Damascus: Institut Français de Damas, 1974.

__________. "Les Documents du Mahkama comme source pour l'histoire economique et sociale de l'Egypte au XVIIIe siècle." In *Les Arabes par leurs Archives: XVIe-XXe Siècles*, ed. Jacques Berque and Dominique Chevalier. Paris: 1976.

__________. "Une liste des corporations des métiers au Caire en 1801." *Arabica* 4(1957):151-63.

__________. "Al-Aḥyā' al-Aristuqrāṭiyyah bi al-Qāhira fī al-Qarn al-Thāmin ᶜAshar." Translated by Zuhayr al-Shāyib. *Al-Majallah* 149 (1969):69-86.

__________. "Al-Aḥyā' al-Qāhirah al-Shaᶜbiyyah fī al-Qarn al-Thāmin ᶜAshar wa al-Harakāt al-Jamāhiriyyah al-Latti Qāmat bihā." Translated by Zuhayr al-Shāyib. *Al-Ṭaliᶜah* 7(1968):46-54.

__________. "Al-Qāhirah al-ᶜUthmāniyyah bi waṣfihā Madīnah." Translated by Zuhayr al-Shāyib. *Al-Majallah al-Tārikhiyyah al-Miṣriyyah* 20(1973):226-29.

Saᶜdāwī, Nazīr H. *Ṣuwar wa Maẓālim min ᶜAṣr al-Mamālīk.* Cairo: Makatabat al-Nahḍah, 1966.

Samī, Amīn. *Tawqīm al-Nīl.* 6 vols. Cairo: Dār al-Kutub, 1928.

Schacht, Joseph. *An Introduction to Islamic Law.* Oxford: Oxford University Press, 1964.

Schacht, Joseph. *The Origins of Muhammadan Jurisprudence*. Oxford: Oxford University Press, 1950.

__________. "Pre-Islamic Background and Early Development of Jurisprudence." In *Law in the Middle East*, ed. M. Khadduri and H.J. Liebesny. Washington: Middle East Institute, 1955.

__________. "The Schools of Law and Later Developments of Jurisprudence." In *Law in the Middle East*, ed. M. Khadduri and H.J. Liebesny. Washington: Middle East Institute, 1955.

Al-Sharqāwī, Maḥmūd. *Miṣr fī al-Qarn al-Thāmin ᶜAshar*. Cairo: Maktabat al-Anjlo, 1957.

Shaw, Stanford J. *The Financial and Administrative Organization and Development of Ottoman Egypt, 1517-1798*. Princeton: Princeton University Press, 1962.

__________. *Ottoman Egypt in the Age of the French Revolution.* Cambridge: Harvard University Press, 1964.

__________. *Ottoman Egypt in the Eighteenth Century: The Nizamname-i Misir of Cezzar Ahmed Pasha*. Cambridge: Harvard University Press, 1962.

__________. *The Budget of Ottoman Egypt, 1005-1006/1596-1597*. The Hague: Mouton, 1968.

__________. "Landholding and Land-Tax Revenues in Ottoman Egypt." In *Political and Social Change in Modern Egypt*, ed. P.M. Holt, pp. 91-103. London: Oxford University Press, 1968.

__________. "The Land Law of Ottoman Egypt (960-1553): A Contribution to the Study of Landholding in the Early Years of Ottoman Rule in Egypt." *Der Islam* 38(1962):106-37.

__________. "Cairo's Archives and the History of Ottoman Egypt." In *Report on Research, Spring 1956*, pp. 59-72. Washington: Middle East Institute, 1956.

__________. "Turkish Source-Materials for Egyptian History." In *Political and Social Change in Modern Egypt*, ed. P.M. Holt, pp. 28-51. London: Oxford University Press, 1968.

Strauss, E. "The Social Isolation of Ahl Adh-Dhimma." *Etudes d'Orient a la Memoire de Paul P. Hirschler* 1(1950):73-94.

Surūr, Muḥammad J. *Dawlat Banī Qalāwūn fī Miṣr: al-Ḥālah al-Siyāsiyyah wa al-Iqtiṣādiyyah fī ᶜAhdihā bi Wajh Khāṣṣ*. Cairo: Dār al-Fikr, 1947.

Tritton, A.S. "Non-Muslim Subjects of the Muslim State." *Journal of the Royal Asiatic Society* 1942:36-40.

Tyan, Emile. *Histoire de l'organisation judiciaire en pays d'Islam.* 2 vols. Leiden: Brill, 1959.

__________. "Judicial Organization." In *Law in the Middle East*, ed. M. Khadduri and H.J. Liebesny. Washington: Middle East Institute, 1955.

Udovitch, Abraham L. *Partnership and Profit in Medieval Islam.* Princeton: Princeton University Press, 1970.

__________. "Theory and Practice of Islamic Law: Some Evidence from the Geniza." *Studia Islamica* 32(1970):289-303.

Wakin, Jeanette A. *The Function of Documents in Islamic Law*. Albany: State University of New York Press, 1972.

Walz, Terence. "Wakalat al-Gallaba: The Market for Sudan Goods in Cairo." *Annales Islamologiques* 3(1977):217-45.

Williams, John A. "The Monuments of Ottoman Cairo." In *Colloque*

International sur l'Histoire du Caire, pp. 453-63. Cairo: Ministry of Culture, 1972.

Woods, John E. *The Aqquyunlu: Clan, Confederation, Empire*. Minneapolis and Chicago: Bibliotheca Islamica, 1976.

Ziadeh, Farhat J. "Urf and Law in Islam." In *The World of Islam: Studies in Honour of P.K. Hitti*, pp. 60-67. London: 1959.

UNPUBLISHED PAPERS

Mīlād, Salwā. "Sijillāt Mahkamat al-Bāb al-ᶜĀlī: Dirāsah Arshīfiyyah Diplūmātiyyah." 2 vols. Ph.D. dissertation, Cairo University, 1975.

Zilfi, Madeline. "The Ottoman Ulema 1703-1829 and the Route to Great Mullaship." Ph.D. dissertation, University of Chicago, 1976.

INDEX

^{c}Abd al-Halim, Muhammad b., 14
administrative law, *cases*, 34-35, *in the registers*, 10
ahl al-khibrah, 22-23, *in inheritance cases*, 48
alcohol, *disputes relating to*, 39
amīn bayt al-māl, 21
amīns, 7
apostasy, *cases*, 28
arbitrators, see *al-muṣliḥūn*
arrests, 21
ashrāf, 33
assault, *cases*, 29, 30, 31
awqāf, *administration*, 68-71, *cases*, 53, 55, 66, 70-71, *istibdāl of*, 16, *rental of properties*, 54, *revised by Ottomans* 7

al-Bāb al-^{c}Ālī, *cases referred to*, 16, *na'ibs at*, 15
bankruptcy, *cases*, 38
berāt, 15
bond, 41, *cases*, 39
building code, 22, *cases*, 57
building inspectors, 52

charges, 21
child support, *cases*, 46
Christians, *cases*, 39, see also non-Muslims
class distinctions, see social classes
collateral, *cases*, 39, 40
complainants, 21
contempt of court, *cases*, 40-41
contracts, *cases*, 22, see also sales
co-signers, *cases*, 39
court registers, 9-11
courts, *located*, 13, *number*, 83, Ch. III, nn.4-5, *structure*, 12-13, 16
crimes, *and the Sharī^{c}ah*, 5, *responsible parties*, 21
criminal law, 25-35, *procedure*, 11
criminal record, 32

defendants, 40
desertion, *cases*, 47
disturbing the peace, *cases*, 27, 53, 55
divorce, 45-46, *cases*, 44-47
dīwān, 15, 91, n. 90
dowry, *cases*, 44

Egyptian society, 11
embezzlement, *cases*, 37
estates, 23, see also inheritance
expert witnesses, see *ahl al-khibrah*

false accusation of fornication, *cases*, 28
faskh, 16
fatwahs, 23
fees, see *rusūm*
fornication, *cases*, 28

ghafīr, 65, 66
governor, provincial, 65
guilds, see *ṭawā'if*

ḥaqq al-ṭarīq, 21-22
ḥājib, 6
Ḥanafi school, 14, 16-17
ḥārah, 52-58
heirs, see inheritance
ḥiwālah, 38, *cases*, 38-39
ḥiyal, 10
ḥujjahs, 18-19, *fees for*, 23, *use in civil cases*, 41
ḥuqūq al-ākharīn, 25
ḥuqūq Allāh, 25

iflās, 16
ījārāt, 16
inheritance, 47-49, 84, n. 9, *use of ahl al-khibrah*, 23
innocence, affirmation of, see *yamīn*
intentional infliction of emotional distress, *case*, 31
interest, 41
investigation, 26-28
*iqṭā*ᶜ, 7
istiḥsān, 5

Jews, 38, 39, 42, see also non-Muslims
judiciary, 7-8, 15-17
justice, *as basis of state power*, 4

kafālah, 41
khūlīs, 65, 66
kiswah, *cases*, 45

leases, 54
loans, *cases*, 36-38, 40-41, 48

mahr, *cases*, 44
Mamluks, 82, n. 34
market regulation, 61, *cases*, 61, *quality control*, 60
marriage contracts, *cases*, 44-46
maṣlaḥah, 6
maẓālim, 6
military, 7, 33, *crimes by*, 34
minimum wage, *examples*, 60
muftīs, 23
muḥḍirs, 20-21
muḥtasib, 6
multazims, 6, 66-67, *non-Muslims as*, 56
murder, 27, *cases*, 27-30
al-muṣliḥūn (al-muslimūn), 19-20

nāhiyyah, 12
nā'ib, 14, 16, *authority of Ḥanafī*, 17
naqīb, 58, 60
nāẓir, 22, 68, 70, see also *awqāf*
neighborhoods, see *ḥārah*
non-Muslims, 33, 38, 42-43, 56, 58, *cases*, 38, 52-53, 57

Ottoman government, 4
Ottoman penal code, 32-34

partnership, *cases*, 37
penalties, 32, 41
personal injury, *cases*, 31, see also assault
plaintiff, *civil*, 36, *criminal*, 25-26
police, 88, n. 53
positive law, 1
pricing, 61
privacy, *cases*, 52-53
procedure, civil, 36
provinces, *administration*, 65, *in Ottoman Egypt*, 82, Ch. III, n. 1
public nuisance, *cases*, 53
punishments, 11

qaḍā', 12
qāḍī, 6, 14, 15, 17, 84, n. 16, *power to bring charges*, 26, *responsibilities in rural administration*, 65
qāḍī ᶜaskar, 6, 13-14
qāḍī al-quḍāh, 13, 84, n. 15, see also *qāḍī ᶜaskar*
qā'im maqām, 13
qānūns, 3, 5-6
qassām, 14, 48
qiṣāṣ, 42-43

rahīnah, 39
ra'īs, 3
rape, *cases*, 30
religious disputes, *cases*, 42, 57

restraint of trade, *cases*, 63
retaliation, 42-43
ribā, 41
rural administration, 65-68
rusūm, 23-24

ṣabīs, 58, 60
sales, *notarized in court*, 10, *cases*, 36-37, 40
ṣanay^{c}īs, 58, 60
sentencing, 32-33
separation of powers, 15
Sharī^{c}ah, 1, *as basis of state power*, 4-5, 72, *and judiciary*, 3, *evidence according to*, 34
shaykh (of the *ṭawā'if)*, 3, 59, *cases*, 58-59
shaykh (of the village), 65 ff., *cases*, 67
shuhūd, 5, 18, 19, 31, *cases challenging*, 30
shurūṭ, 10
shurtah, 6, see also police
al-siyāsah al-shar^{c}iyyah, 6
slaves, 49
social classes, 2, 51
subashi, 33, *abuse of powers, case*, 34
sultan, *as source of power*, 15
sunnah, 5
sūq, 61

ṭawā'if, 2-3, 54, 57-64, *in inheritance cases*, 48, *members as ahl al-khibrah*, 22-23, *non-Muslims in*, 56
taxes, 51, *cases*, 62, 67-68, *collection procedure*, 67
testimony, 28-31
theft, *cases*, 30
tradition, see *sunnah*
treasury, *rights in inheritance*, 47-49
trials, *procedure*, 28-31

^{c}udūl, 10, 18-19, 26-27, 48, 52, 67, *report as decisive, cases*, 30
^{c}udūl al-nāḥiyyah, 19
^{c}Umar, 5
^{c}urf, 5
usṭahs, 58, 60

verbal assault, *cases*, 29

wage, minimum, 60
wakālahs, 61
wakil, 25-26, 36, 48, 67, *cases*, 29, 44, *for women*, 51, *non-Muslims as*, 51, *women as*, 36
wālī, 7, 26
waqf, see *awqāf*
waqfiyyah, 68-69
witnesses, 24, see also *^{c}udūl*, *al-muṣliḥūn*, and *shuhūd*
women, 49-40, 55, see also divorce, marriage contracts

Yaḥyā b. Zakariyyā, 14
yamīn, 30, 31, *cases*, 37, 38, 47, 48

ẕimmis, see non-Muslims

[redacted]